Manners, Customs, and History

of the

Highlanders of Scotland

&

Historical Account

of the

Clan MacGregor

Sir Walter Scott

This edition published by Barnes & Noble, Inc.

1993 Barnes & Noble Books

ISBN 1-56619-150-5
Printed and bound in the United States of America

M 9 8 7 6 5 4 3 2

MANNERS, CUSTOMS, AND HISTORY OF THE HIGHLANDERS OF SCOTLAND.

CONTENTS.

Contents.

Contents.

Contents.

HISTORICAL ACCOUNT OF THE CLAN MACGREGOR.

CONTENTS.

Contents.

Contents.

ADVERTISEMENT.—These two little-known works of Sir
Walter Scott's were originally published in the *Quarterly
Review*, and have seldom been re-published.

MANNERS, CUSTOMS, AND HISTORY

OF THE

HIGHLANDERS OF SCOTLAND.

CHAPTER I.

Ignorance regarding the Highlands—The Pretender and the Highlanders—Battle of Prestonpans—Advance into England—Retreat
—Battle of Culloden.

EVERYTHING belonging to the Highlands of Scotland
has of late become peculiarly interesting. It is not
much above a half a century since it was otherwise.
The inhabitants of the lowlands of Scotland were, indeed, aware that there existed, in the extremity of the
island, amid wilder mountains and broader lakes than
their own, tribes of men called clans, living each under
the rule of their own chief, wearing a peculiar dress,
speaking an unknown language, and going armed even
in the most ordinary and peaceful vocation.

The more southern counties saw specimens of these
men, following the droves of cattle which were the
sole exportable commodity of their country, plaided,
bonneted, belted and brogued, and driving their
bullocks, as Virgil is said to have spread his manure,

with an air of great dignity and consequence. To
their nearer Lowland neighbours, they were known by
more fierce and frequent causes of acquaintance; by
the forays which they made upon the inhabitants of
the plains, and the tribute, or protection-money, which
they exacted from those whose possessions they spared.

But in England, the knowledge of the very existence
of the Highlanders was, prior to 1745, faint and forgotten; and not even the recollection of those civil
wars which they had maintained in the years 1689,
1715, and 1719, had made much impression on the
British public. The more intelligent, when they
thought of them by any chance, considered them as
complete barbarians; and the mass of the people cared
no more about them than the merchants of New York
about the Indians who dwell beyond the Alleghany
mountains. Swift, in his *Journal to Stella*, mentions
having dined in company with two gentlemen from the
Highlands of Scotland, and expresses his surprise at
finding them persons of ordinary decorum and civility.

Such was the universal ignorance of the rest of the
island respecting the inhabitants of this remote corner
of Britain, when the events of the remarkable years
1745-6 roused them, " like a rattling peal of thunder."
On the 25th of July, 1745, the eldest son of the
Chevalier Saint George, usually called from that circumstance the young Chevalier, landed in Moidart, in
the West Highlands, with seven attendants only; and
his presence was sufficient to summon about eighteen

hundred men to his standard, even before the news of his arrival could reach London. This little army was composed of a few country gentlemen, acting as commanders of battalions raised from the peasants or commoners of their estates, and officered by the principal farmers, or tacksmen. None of them pretended to knowledge of military affairs, and very few had ever seen an action.

With such adequate forces, the adventurer marched forward, like the hero of romance, to prove his fortune. The most considerable part of the regular army moved to meet him at the pass of Corry-arrack; and, as we learn from the Culloden papers, the Chevalier called for his Highland dress, and, tying the latchet of a pair of Highland brogues, swore he would fight the army of the government before he unloosed them. But Sir John Cope, avoiding an action, marched to Inverness, leaving the low countries open to the Chevalier, who instantly rushed down on them; and while one part of the government army retreated northward to avoid him, he chased before him the remainder, which fled to the south. He crossed the Forth on the 13th September, and in two days afterwards was master of the metropolis of Scotland.

The king's forces having again united at Dunbar, and being about to advance upon Edinburgh, sustained at Prestonpans one of the most complete defeats recorded in history, their cavalry flying in irretrievable confusion, and all their infantry being killed or made prisoners.

Under these auspices, the Highland army, now about five or six thousand strong, advanced into England although Marshal Wade lay at Newcastle with one army and the Duke of Cumberland was at the head of another in the centre of the kingdom. They took Carlisle, a walled town, with a castle of considerable strength, and struck a degree of confusion and terror into the public mind, at which those who witnessed and shared it were afterwards surprised and ashamed. London, says a contemporary, writing on the spur of the moment, lies open as a prize to the first comers, whether Scotch or Dutch; and a letter from Gray to Horace Walpole, paints an indifference yet more ominous to the public cause than the general panic :— " the common people in town at least know how to be afraid; but we are such uncommon people here (at Cambridge) as to have no more sense of danger than if the battle had been fought where and when the battle of Cannæ was.—I heard three sensible middle-aged men, when the Scotch were said to be at Stamford, and actually were at Derby, talking of hiring a chaise to go to Caxton (a place in the high-road) to see the Pretender and Highlanders as they passed."

A further evidence of the feelings under which the public laboured during this crisis, is to be found in a letter from the well-known Sir Andrew Mitchell to the Lord President.

" If I had not lived long enough in England to know the natural bravery of the people, particularly of the better sort, I should, from their behaviour of late, have had a very false opinion of them ; for the least scrap of good news exalts them most absurdly ; and the smallest reverse of fortune depresses them meanly."

In fact the alarm was not groundless ;—not that the number of the Chevalier's individual followers ought to have been an object of serious, at least of permanent alarm to so great a kingdom,—but because, in many counties, a great proportion of the landed interest were Jacobitically disposed, although, with the prudence which distinguished the opposite party in 1688, they declined joining the invaders until it should appear whether they could maintain their ground without them. If it had rested with the unfortunate but daring leader of this strange adventure, his courage, though far less supported either by actual strength of numbers or by military experience, was as much " screwed to the sticking-place " as that of the Prince of Orange.

The history of the council of war, at Derby, in which Charles Edward's retreat was determined, has never yet been fully explained ; it will, however, be one day made known ;—in the meantime, it is proved that no cowardice on his part, no wish to retreat from the desperate adventure in which he was engaged, and to shelter himself from its consequences, dictated the movement which was then adopted. *Vestigia nulla retrorsum* had been his motto from the beginning. When retreat was determined upon, contrary to his arguments, entreaties, and tears, he evidently con-

sidered his cause as desperate : he seemed, in many
respects, an altered man ; and from being the leader of
his little host, became in appearance, as he was in
reality, their reluctant follower.   While the Highland
army advanced, Charles was always in the van by the
break of day ;—in retreat, his alacrity was gone, and
often they were compelled to wait for him ;—he lost
his spirit, his gaiety, his hardihood, and he never regained them but when battle was spoken of.   In later
life, when all hopes of re-establishment were ended,
Charles Edward sunk into frailties by which he was
debased and dishonoured.

But let us be just to the memory of the unfortunate.
Without courage, he had never made the attempt—
without address and military talent, he had never kept
together his own desultory bands, or discomfited the
more experienced soldiers of his enemy ;—and finally,
without patience, resolution, and fortitude, he could
never have supported his cause so long, under successive
disappointments, or fallen at last with honour, by an
accumulated and overwhelming pressure.

When the resolution of retreat was adopted, it was
accomplished with a dexterous celerity, as remarkable
as the audacity of the advance.   With Ligonier's army
on one flank, and Cumberland's in the rear—surrounded
by hostile forces,—and without one hope remaining of
countenance or assistance from the Jacobites of England, the Highlanders made their retrograde movement
without either fear or loss, and had the advantage at

Clifton, near Penrith, in the only skirmish which took place between them and their numerous pursuers. The same good fortune seemed for a time to attend the continuation of the war, when removed once more to Scotland. The Chevalier, at the head of his little army, returned to the north more like a victor than a retreating adventurer. He laid Glasgow under ample contribution, refreshed and collected his scattered troops, and laid siege to Stirling, whose castle guards the principal passage between the Highlands and Lowlands.

In the meanwhile, General Hawley was sent against him; an officer so confident of success, that he declared he would trample the Highland insurgents into dust with only two regiments of dragoons; and whose first order, on entering Edinburgh, was to set up a gibbet in the Grass Market, and another between Leith and Edinburgh. But this commander received from his despised opponents so sharp a defeat, at Falkirk, that, notwithstanding all the colours which could be put upon it, the affair appeared not much more creditable than that of Prestonpans. How Hawley looked upon this occasion, we learn by a letter from General Wightman.

"General H——y is in much the same situation as General C—e : he was never seen in the field during the battle; and everything would have gone to wreck, in a worse manner than at Preston, if General Huske had not acted with judgment and courage, and appeared everywhere. H——y seems to be sensible of his misconduct ; for when I was with him on Saturday morning at Linlithgow, he looked most wretchedly ; even worse than C—e did a few hours after his scuffle, when I saw him at Fala."

Even when the approach of the Duke of Cumberland, with a predominant force, compelled these adventurers to retreat towards their northern recesses, they were so far from being disheartened that they generally had the advantage in the sort of skirmishing warfare which preceded their final defeat at Culloden. On this occasion, they seem, for the first time, to have laboured under a kind of judicial infatuation. They did not defend the passage of Spey, though broad, deep, rapid, and dangerous ; they did not retreat before the Duke into the defiles of their own mountains, where regular troops pursuing them could not long have subsisted ; they did not even withdraw two leagues, which would have placed them in a position inaccessible to horse and favourable to their own mode of fighting : they did not await their own reinforcements, although three thousand men, a number equal to one half of their army, were within a day's march. But, on the contrary, they wasted the spirits of their people, already exhausted by hunger and dispirited by retreat, in a forced march, with the purpose of a night attack, which was hastily and rashly adopted, and as inconsiderately abandoned ; and at length drew up in an open plain, exposed to the fire of artillery, and protected from the charge of cavalry only by a park wall, which was soon pulled down. This they did, though they themselves had no efficient force of either description: and in such a hopeless position they awaited the encounter of an enemy more than double their numbers, fully equipped, and in a complete state for battle. The result was what might have been expected—the loss, namely, of all but their honour, which was well maintained, since they left nearly the half of their army upon the field.

What causes, at this critical period, distracted those councils which had hitherto exhibited sagacity and military talent, it would be difficult now to ascertain. An officer, deep in their counsels, offers no better reason than that they must have expected a continuation of the same miraculous success which had hitherto befriended them against all probable calculation and chance of war—a sort of crowning mercy, as Cromwell might have called it, granted to the supposed goodness of their cause, and their acknowledged courage, in defiance of all the odds against them. But we believe the truth to be, that the French advisers who were around the Chevalier had, by this time, the majority in his councils. They were alarmed at the prospect of a mountain war, which presented a long perspective of severe hardship and privation; and being, at the worst, confident of their own safety as prisoners of war, they urged the adventurer to stand this fearful hazard, which, as we all know, terminated in utter and irremediable defeat.

CHAPTER II.

Peculiarities of Clan government and Highland habits—Revengeful Disposition—The Muat and Cameron Feud—The Lesley and Leith fight—Characteristics of Highland Chiefs—Nature of the customs as conducive of tribal divisions—Distinctive Appelatives of the Chiefs.

IT was not till after these events, which we have hastily retraced, that the Highlanders, with the peculiarity of their government and habits, became a general object of attention and investigation. And evidently it must have been matter of astonishment to the subjects of the complicated and combined constitution of Great Britain, to find they were living at the next door to tribes whose government and manners were simply and purely patriarchal, and who, in the structure of their social system, much more resembled the inhabitants of the mountains of India than those of the plains of England. Indeed, when we took up the account of Cabul, lately published by the Honourable Mr. Elphinstone, we were forcibly struck with the curious points of parallelism between the manners of the Afghan tribes and those of the ancient Highland clans.

They resembled these Oriental mountaineers in their feuds, in their adoption of auxiliary tribes, in their laws, in their modes of conducting war, in their arms, and, in some respects, even in their dress. A Highlander who made the *amende honorable* to an enemy, came to his dwelling, laid his head upon the block, or offered him his sword held by the point; an Afghan does the

same. It was deemed unworthy, in either case, to refuse the clemency implored, but it might be legally done. We recollect an instance in Highland history:—
William Macintosh, a leader, if not the chief, of that ancient clan, upon some quarrel with the Gordons, burnt the castle of Auchindown, belonging to this powerful family; and was, in the feud which followed, reduced to such extremities by the persevering vengeance of the Earl of Huntly, that he was at length compelled to surrender himself at discretion. He came to the castle of Strathbogie, choosing his time when the earl was absent, and yielded himself up to the countess. She informed him that Huntly had sworn never to forgive him the offence he had committed, until he should see his head upon the block. The humbled chieftain kneeled down, and laid his head upon the kitchen dresser, where the oxen were cut up for the baron's feast. No sooner had he made this humiliation, than the cook, who stood behind him with his cleaver uplifted, at a sign from the inexorable countess, severed Macintosh's head from his body at a stroke.

So deep was this thirst of vengeance impressed on the minds of the Highlanders, that when a clergyman informed a dying chief of the unlawfulness of the sentiment, urged the necessity of his forgiving an inveterate enemy, and quoted the scriptural expression, " Vengeance is mine, saith the Lord," the acquiescing penitent said, with a deep sigh,

" To be sure, it is too sweet a morsel for a mortal."

Then added, " Well, I forgive him ; but the deil take you, Donald " (turning to his son), " if *you* forgive him."

Another extraordinary instance occurred in Aberdeenshire. In the sixteenth century, Muat of Abergeldie, then a powerful baron, made an agreement to meet with Cameron of Brux, with whom he was at feud, each being attended with twelve *horse* only. But Muat, treacherously taking advantage of the literal meaning of the words, came with two riders on each horse. They met at Drumgaudrum, a hill near the river Don ; and in the unequal conflict which ensued, Brux fell, with most of his friends. The estate descended to an only daughter, Katherine ; whose hand the widowed Lady Brux, with a spirit well suited to the times, offered as a reward to any one who would avenge her husband's death. Robert Forbes, a younger son of the chief of that family, undertook the adventure ; and having challenged Muat to single combat, fought with and slew him at a place called Badenyon, near the head of Glenbucket. A stone called Clachmuat (*i.e.*, Muat's stone) still marks the place of combat. When the victor presented himself to claim the reward of his valour, and to deprecate any delay of his happiness, Lady Brux at once cut short all ceremonial, by declaring that " Kate Cameron should go to Robert Forbes's bed while Muat's blood was yet reeking upon his gully " (*i.e.*, knife). The victor expressed no disapprobation of this arrangement, nor did the maiden scruples of the bride impede her filial obedience.*

One more example (and we could add an hundred) of that insatiable thirst for revenge, which attended northern feuds.   One of the Leslies, a strong and active young man, chanced to be in company with a number of the clan of Leith, the feudal enemies of his own.   The place where they met being the hall of a powerful and neutral neighbour, Leslie was, like Shakespeare's Tybalt in a similar situation, compelled to endure their presence.   Still he held the opinion of the angry Capulet, even in the midst of the entertainment,

> " Now by the stock and honour of my kin,
>   To strike him dead I hold it not a sin."

Accordingly, when they stood up to dance, and he found himself compelled to touch the hands and approach the persons of his detested enemies, the deadly feud broke forth.   He unsheathed his dagger as he went down the dance—struck on the right and left—laid some dead and many wounded on the floor—threw up the window, leaped into the castle-court, and escaped in the general confusion.   Such were the unsettled principles of the time, that the perfidy of the action was lost in its boldness ; it was applauded by

* Vide note to " Don," a poem, reprinted by Moir, Edinburgh, 1816, from an edition in 1742.

his kinsmen, who united themselves to defend what he had done; and the fact is commemorated in the well-known tune of triumph called *Lesly among the Leiths.*

The genealogies of the Afghan tribes may be paralleled with those of the clans; the nature of their favourite sports, their love of their native land, their hospitality, their address, their simplicity of manners exactly correspond. Their superstitions are the same, or nearly so. The *Gholée Beabaun* (demons of the desert) resemble the *Boddach* of the Highlanders, who "walked the heath at midnight and at noon." The Afghan's most ordinary mode of divination is by examining the marks in the blade-bone of a sheep, held up to the light; and even so the Rev. Mr. Robert Kirk assures us, that in his time, the end of the sixteenth century, "the seers prognosticate many future events (only for a month's space) from the shoulder-bone of a sheep on which a knife never came. By looking into the bone, they will tell if whoredom be committed in the owner's house; what money the master of the sheep had; if any will die out of that house for a month, and if any cattle there will take a *trake* (*i.e.* a disease), as if planet-struck.*

The Afghan, who, in his weary travels, had seen no vale equal to his own native valley of Speiger, may

* Essay on the Nature and Actions of the subterranean invisible people, going under the names of Elves, Fairies, and the like. London, 1815.

find a parallel in many an exile from the braes of Loch-aber; and whoever had remonstrated with an ancient Highland chief, on the superior advantages of a civilized life regulated by the authority of equal laws, would have received an answer something similar to the indignant reply of the old Afghan; " We are content with discord, we are content with alarms, we are content with blood, but we will never be content with a master." * The Highland chiefs, otherwise very frequently men of sense and education, and only dis-tinguished in Lowland society by an affectation of rank and stateliness, somewhat above their means, were, in their own country, from the absolute submission paid to them by their clans, and the want of frequent inter-course with persons of the same rank with themselves, nursed in a high and daring spirit of independent sovereignty which would not brook or receive pro-tection or control from the public law or government; and disdained to owe their possessions and the preser-vation of their rights to any thing but their own broad-swords.

Similar examples may be derived from the history of Persia by Sir John Malcolm. But our limits do not permit us further to pursue a parallel which serves strikingly to show how the same state of society and civilisation produces similar manners, laws, and customs, even at the most remote periods of time, and in the

* Account of Cabul, 174, Note.

most distant quarters of the world. In two respects
the manners of the Cabul tribes differ materially from
those of the Highlanders; first, in the influence of their
Jeergas, or patriarchal senates, which diminishes the
power of their chiefs, and gives a democratic turn to
each separate tribe. This appears to have been a perpetual and radical difference; for at no time do the
Highland chiefs appear to have taken counsel with
their elders, as an authorized and independent body,
although, no doubt, they availed themselves of their
advice and experience, upon the principle of a general
who summons a council of war. This is to be understood generally; for there were circumstances in which
the subordinate chieftains of the clan took upon them
to control the chief, as when the Mackenzies forcibly
compelled the Earl of Seaforth to desist from his purpose of pulling down his family-seat of castle Brahan.
The second point of distinction respects the consolida-
tion of those detached tribes under one head, or
king, who, with a degree of authority greater or
less according to his talents, popularity, and other
circumstances, is the acknowledged head of the
associated communities. In this point, however, the
Highlanders anciently resembled the Afghans, as will
appear when we give a brief sketch of their general
history. But this, to be intelligible, must be preceded
by some account of their social system, of which the
original and primitive basis differed very little from the

first time that we hear of them in history until the destruction of clanship in 1748.

The Scottish Highlanders were, like the Welsh, the unmixed aboriginal natives of the island, speaking a dialect of the ancient Celtic, once the language of all Britain, and being the descendants of those tribes which had been driven by the successive invasions of nations more politic than themselves, and better skilled in the regular arts of war, into the extensive mountainous tract which, divided by an imaginary line, drawn from Dunbarton, includes both sides of Loch Lomond, and the higher and more mountainous parts of Stirling and Perthshire, Angus, Mearns, and Aberdeenshire. Beyond this line all the people speak Gaelic, and wear, or did wear, the Highland dress. The Western Islands are comprehended within this wild and extensive territory, which includes upwards of two hundred parishes, and a population of about two hundred thousand souls.

The country, though in many places so wild and savage as to be almost uninhabitable, contains on the sea-coasts, on the sides of the lakes, in the vales of the small streams, and in the more extensive *straths* through which larger rivers discharge themselves, much arable ground; and the mountains which surround these favoured spots afford ample pasture walks, and great abundance of game. Natural forests of oak, fir, and birch, are found in most places of the country, and were anciently yet more extensive. These glens, or valleys, were each the domain of a separate tribe, who lived for each other, laboured in common, married usually within the clan, and, the passages from one vale to another being dangerous in most seasons, and toilsome in all, had very little communication with the world beyond their own range of mountains.

This circumstance doubtless tended to prolong among these separate tribes a species of government, the first that is known in the infancy of society, and which, in most instances, is altered or modified during an early period of its progress. The chief himself had a separate appellative, formed on the same principle: thus the chief of the Campbells was called MacCallam-more (*i.e.* the son of the great Colin); Glengarry is called MacAllister-more, and so forth. Their language has no higher expression of rank; and when the family of Slate were ennobled, their clansmen could only distinguish *Lord* MacDonald as MacDhonuil-more (*i.e.* the great MacDonald). To this was often added some special epithet distinguishing the individual or reigning chief. Thus, John Duke of Argyle was called *Jan Roy nan Cath*, as the celebrated Viscount of Dundee was termed *Jan Dhu nan Cath*, namely, *Red* or Black John of the Battles. Such epithets distinguished one chief from another, but the patronymic of the dynasty was common to all.

CHAPTER III.

Obedience to the Chiefs—Three Classes—Chiefs Tacksmen, etc, and Common People—Succession and Inheritance—The difference between Chiefs and Chieftains—Pride of Lineage—Characteristics and Duties of the Tacksmen—The Common Dependence—Over Population and its Consequences—The Younger Sons—Military Spirit and Eternal Feuds Among the Clans.

THE obedience of the Highlander was paid to the chief of his clan, as representing some remote ancestor from whom it was supposed the whole tribe was originally descended, and whose name, compounded into a patronymic, as we have already mentioned, was the distinguishing appellation of the sept. Each clan, acting upon this principle, bore to its chief all the zeal, all the affectionate deference, all the blind devotion, of children to a father. Their obedience was grounded on the same law of nature, and a breach of it was regarded as equally heinous. The clansmen who scrupled to save his chief's life at the expense of his own, was regarded as a coward who fled from his father's side in the hour of peril. Upon this simple principle rests the whole doctrine of clanship; and although the authority of the chief sometimes assumed a more legal aspect, as the general law of the country then stood, by his being possessed of feudal influence, or territorial jurisdiction—yet, with his clan, no feudal rights, or magisterial authority, could enhance or render more ample that power which he possessed, *jure sanguinis*, by the right of primogeniture. The duty of the clansman was indelible; and no feudal grant which he might acquire, or other engagement whatever, was to be preferred to his service to the chief. In the following letter Mac-Intoshe summons, as his rightful followers, those of his people who were resident on the estate of Culloden, who, according to low country law, ought to have followed their landlord.

" MADAM,

" You can'nt be a Stranger to the Circumstances I have put myself in at the tyme, and the great need I have of my own men & followers wherever they may be found. Wherfor I thought fitt, seeing Cullodin is not at home, by this line to intreat you to put no stopp in the way of these Men that are & have been my followers upon your Ground.

" Madam, your compliance in this will very much oblige,

" Your most humble Servant,

" L. MACINTOSHE.

" 14th Sept. 1715.

" Madam,

" P.S. If what I demand will not be granted, I hope I'll be excused to be in my duty."

Such was the very simple theory of clan-government. In practice, it extended farther. Each clan was divided into three orders. The head of all was the CHIEF, who was usually, though not uniformly, the proprietor of all, or the greater part of the territories of the clan; not, it must be supposed, in absolute property, but as the head and grand steward of the community. He administered them, however, in all respects, at his own will and pleasure. A certain portion of the best of the land he retained as his own appanage, and it was cultivated for his sole profit. The rest was divided by grants, of a nature more or less temporary, among the second class of the clan, who are called TENANTS, TACKSMEN, or GOODMEN. These were the near relations of the chief, or were descended from those who bore such near relation to some of his ancestors. To each of these, brothers, nephews, cousins, and so forth, the chief assigned a portion of land, either during pleasure, or upon short lease, or frequently in the form of a *wadset* (mortgage), redeemable for a certain sum of money.

These small portions of land, assisted by the liberality of their relations, the tacksmen contrived to stock, and on these they subsisted, until in a generation or two the lands were resumed for portioning out some nearer relative, and the descendants of the original tacksman sunk into the situation of commoners. This was such an ordinary transition, that the third class, consisting of the common people, was strengthened in the principle on which their clannish obedience depended, namely, their belief in their original connexion of the genealogy of the chief, since each generation saw a certain number of families merge among the commoners whom their fathers had ranked among the tacksmen or nobility of the clan.

This change, though frequent, did not uniformly take place. In the case of a very powerful chief, or of one who had an especial affection for a son or brother, a portion of land was assigned to a cadet in perpetuity, or he was perhaps settled in an appanage conquered from some other clan, or the tacksman acquired wealth and property by marriage, or by some exertion of his own. In all these cases he kept his rank in society, and usually had under his government a branch or subdivision of the tribe, who looked up to him as their immediate leader, and whom he governed with the same authority and in the same manner, in all respects, as the chief, who was patriarchal head of the whole sept. Such head of a subordinate branch of a clan was called a *chieftain* (a word of distinct and limited meaning), but remained dependent and usually tributary to the *chief*, and bound to support, follow, and obey him in all lawful and unlawful service.

The larger clans often comprehended several of these subdivisions, each of which had its own chieftain; and it sometimes happened when the original family became extinct, that it was difficult to determine the right of succession. This was a calamitous event, for it usually occasioned a civil war; and it was accounted a dishonourable one, since a clan without an acknowledged head was considered an anomaly among them. To use to any member of a clan which chanced to be in this situation the expression, "*Name your chief*," was an insult which nothing but blood could avenge. See *Letters from the North of Scotland*, a work containing much curious information on the former state of the Highlands. The author was Mr. Burt, an engineer, and the work was first published in 1754, thirty years after most of the letters were written. The book has been lately reprinted; and as it contains the observations of an impartial, and, on the whole, an unprejudiced stranger, it is a good record of Highland manners at the commencement of the 18th century. This peculiarity, which, in the course of ages, often took place, was one great source of war among the Highland clans.

When the direct lineage of a chief of an extended lineage became extinct, there arose disputes among the subordinate branches concerning the right of succession to this high dignity. Of these rival chieftains (we use the word in its limited signification), each had his separate band of devoted followers, and, like princes in the same situation, none lacked his *seannachies*, or genealogists to vouch for his title. It is a complete proof of the uncertainty of Highland succession that when a clan regiment was raised, there was a great diversity of opinion who was entitled to the post of honour after the chief, whether the representative of the eldest or of the youngest branch; and as this was a point undecided in the year 1745 (see Home's *History of the Rebellion*, p. 9), it cannot be doubted that so important a difference must repeatedly have drawn blood during the frequent quarrels of ambitious chieftains.

To return to the more simple state of the Highland

clan, in which we suppose the chief to have had no
subordinate leaders approaching to him in degree : his
immediate dependents were the tacksmen, a race of
men upon whose peculiar manners, much rather than
on those of the chief who usually had the advantage
either of an English or French education, or upon the
commons, whose manners, as in all other countries, reflected imperfectly, like a coarse mirror, the habits of
their superiors, the distinct character of the Highlanders rested.   These tacksmen were, by profession,
gentlemen, or, as they termed it in their language,
Duinhé Wassal.   Of this distinction, usually marked
by a feather in the bonnet, for in all other particulars
their dress and that of the chief himself differed little
from that of the commoners, they were especially tenacious ; and the danger of contesting it was the greater,
the nearer the duinhé wassal approached to the state
of the commoner, which was the grave of all the
Capulets.

Wo betide the Lowlander who scrupled to pay the
homage due to the genealogy of a Highland gentleman, even when he condescended to drive his own
cows to market !   When the low country drovers and
graziers met their Highland customers at the trysts of
Donne, and elsewhere on the borders, affronts were
sometimes offered on the one hand, and on the other
the claymore made its instant appearance.   The Lowlanders (we have been assured from those concerned
in such affrays) were less abashed at the display of

steel than might be supposed ; for at the first signal of quarrel they were wont to dip their bonnets in the next rivulet, which, twisted round a stout cudgel, made a tough guard for the hand; and with this precaution both parties were ready to engage—

> " One arm'd with metal, t'other with wood,
> This fit for bruise, and that for blood ;
> With many a stiff thwack, many a bang,
> Hard crab-tree and old iron rang."

The Highlanders had, indeed, the advantage of fire-arms, but rarely used them on such occasions, where a few slashes and broken heads usually decided the combat. Sterner consequences, however, sometimes ensued—these Highland gentlemen were proud in proportion to their poverty, and the quarrels between them and the similar dependants of other families, when they met at the *aqua-vitœ* houses, which were common in this country, gave rise to frequent bloodshed, and often to deadly feuds, between the clans to which the contending parties belonged.

In their intercourse with their respective chiefs, and with the commons, or bulk of the clan, the tacksmen had a double part to play, which demanded all the capacity of skilful courtiers. It was their business to get from both sides as much as they could—from the chief they gained their ends, by means of acting the part of counsellors, assistants, flatterers,—in short, by going through the whole routine of court-intrigue. The exercise of their talents in this, as well as in the

exterior relations of the clan, and its public business, as
it might be called, arising from alliances, jealousies,
feuds, predatory aggressions, and retaliations, was accompanied by the usual effect of sharpening the intellect. The tacksmen accordingly were remarkable for
a ready and versatile politeness in common conversa-
tion, and for a somewhat ostentatious display of the
virtue of hospitality, which was balanced by their art
and address in making bargains, by audacity to demand, eloquence to support their request, and address
to take advantage even of the slightest appearance of
concession. As they had on the one hand to act as a
kind of ministry to the chief, so, on the other, it was
their business to make as much as they could of the
commoners subjected to their immediate jurisdiction;
whom they repaid for their own exactions by protect-
ing them against those which were offered from any
other quarter.

The commons, from hard and scanty fare probably,
were usually inferior in stature to the chiefs, chieftains,
and tacksmen, but extremely hardy and active. They
were supported thus: each tacksman, individually,
leased out his part of the clan territory, in small portions and for moderate rents, to the commoners of the
clan; or by a mode of cultivation often practised on
the continent, and known in Scottish law by the name
of *Steel-bow*, he furnished such a portion of the ground
with stock and seed-corn, on condition of receiving
from the tenant or actual labourer a moiety of the

profits. In either case, the dependence of the cottager
or commoner on the tacksman was as absolute as that
of the tacksman upon the chief, and the general opinion
inculcated upon all was implicit duty to their patriarchal head and his constituted authorities.

This system, in an early state of society, and in a
fertile and uninhabited country, as it is the most obvious,
is also the best which could be adopted. In such a
case, when the flocks and herds of two tribes, like those
of Abraham and Lot, become too numerous for the land
in which they dwell, one kinsman can say to another,
" Why should there be strife between us? Is not the
whole land before thee—separate thyself." But the
most remarkable part of the Highland system, was the
rapid increase of population, which, pent up within
narrow and unfertile valleys, could neither extend itself
towards the mountains, on account of hostile clans, nor
towards the Lowlands, because the civilized country,
though unable to prevent occasional depredations, was
always too powerful to admit of any permanent settlement being gained upon the plains by the mountaineers.
Thus, limited to its own valley, each clan increased in
numbers in a degree far beyond proportion to the means
of supporting them. Each little farm was, by the tenant
who cultivated it, divided and subdivided among his
children and grand-children until the number of human
beings to be maintained far exceeded that for whom,
by any mode of culture, the space of ground could
supply nourishment. We have evidence before us,

that in the rugged district between Loch Katrine and Loch Lomond, in the neighbourhood of Inversnaid, there were one hundred and fifty families living upon ground which did not pay ninety pounds a-year of rent, or, in other words, *each family, at a medium, rented lands at twelve shillings a-year*, as their sole mode of livelihood.

The consequence of this over-population, in any case, must have been laziness, because, where there were so many hands for such light work, none would work hard; and those who could set up the slightest claim of exemption, would not work at all.   This was particularly the case with the tacksmen's younger sons,—a race destined to sink into the insignificance of commoners, unless they could keep themselves afloat by some deed of gallant distinction.   These, therefore, were most afraid of being confounded with the class to which they were provisionally liable to be reduced; and as a serjeant is prouder of his cheveron than an officer of his epaulet, they were eager to maintain their dignity by evincing a contempt of all the duties of peaceful industry, and manifesting their adroitness in the chase and in military exercises. They naturally associated to themselves the stoutest and most active of the youthful commoners, all of whom reckoned their pedigree up to that of the chief, and therefore were entitled to " disdain the shepherd's slothful life." Under such leaders they often committed creaghs, or depredations, on the Lowlands, or on hostile clans, and sometimes constituted themselves into regular bands of robbers, whom the chief connived at, though he dared not openly avow their depredations. They usually found shelter in some remote glen, from which he could, as occasion demanded, let them slip against his enemies. If they were made prisoners, they seldom betrayed the countenance which they had from their protector. On the other hand, he was conscientious in affording them his protection against the law, as far as could be done, without absolutely committing himself.

There yet remained for the younger sons, both of chiefs and tacksmen, another resource, and that was foreign service. From an early period, many of these adventurers sought employment in the continental wars, and after the exile of the House of Stuart, the practice became general. They used also to carry with them some of the most courageous and active of the commoners; thus their acquaintance with actual war, its dangers and its duties, was familiarly maintained, and the report of their adventures and success served to keep up the love of warfare which characterised the Highland clans.

The same military spirit and contempt of labour distinguished even the very lowest of the commoners, upon whom necessarily devolved the operations of agriculture, which were summed up in the arts of ploughing or digging their ground for crops of oats or barley, making hay, rearing cattle, and manufacturing cheese and butter. The labour of the spade and plough was thrown as much as possible on the aged, or females of the clan, while those who were in full vigour of body abandoned themselves alternately to the indulgence of indolence, and to the excitation of violent exercise. And as the tacksmen endeavoured to secure to themselves as large a portion as possible of the produce of the commoner's labour, the latter, to secure his attachment, was indulged and protected in occasional acts of military depredation and license; for which the eternal feuds among the Highlanders themselves, as well as the grand subsisting distinction between them and the Lowlanders, never failed to afford sufficient pretexts.

The last were indeed, on all hands, regarded as the common enemy and general prey, as appears from a letter of apology written by Allan Cameron of Lochiel, to Sir James Grant, chieftain of that name, dated 18th October, 1645. It would seem that a party of Camerons had plundered, or attempted to plunder, the lands of Grant of Moynes, lying on the border of the lowland county of Murray. The Grants had overpowered and worsted the invaders, which did not prevent their chief from remonstrating with Lochiel. Lochiel's answer is in the note, in which it will be observed that the intended robbery of the Murray-man is treated as a matter of course. The only thing requiring apology was the aggression on an allied and friendly clan.

"RIGHT LOVING COUSIN,—My hearty recommendations being remembered to your honour, I have received your honour's letter concerning this misfortunate accident that never fell out, betwixt our houses, the like before, in no man's days; but, praised be God, I am innocent of the same, and my friends both in respect that they gi't (went) not within your honour's bounds, but (only) to Murray-land, *where all men take their prey;* nor knew not that Moynes was a grant, but thought that he was a Murray-man; and if they knew him, they would not stir his land more than the rest of your honour's bounds in Strathspey.—Sir, I have gotten such a loss of my friends, which I hope your honour will consider, for I have eight dead already, and I have twelve or thirteen under cure, whilk I know not who shall live, or who shall die, of the same.   So, sir, who-soever has gotten the greatest loss, I am content that the same be repaired, to (at) the sight of friends that loveth us both alike—and there is such a trouble here among us, that we cannot look to the same, for the present time, while (until) I wit who shall live of my men that is under cure.   So not further troubling your honour at this time, for your honour shall not be offended at my friend's innocence,—Sir, I rest yours,

"ALLAN CAMERON of Lochiel."

CHAPTER IV.

Highland artisans—Great hardihood among all classes—Over-population, want, and starvation—Disposition of the people—Story of
MacDonald of Keppoch—Story of the Chief of Clanronald—
Relationship of chiefs and commoners—The merging of clans and
individuals with other clans—Highland independence of Parlia-
mentary law.

THE artisans in a Highland tribe were few, but rose in rank above the mere labourers of the ground—the women were the principal weavers, but the tailor's was a masculine employment, and as much skill was supposed to be necessary to his craft, he held some importance in society. Every man made his own brogues out of raw hides, and was therefore his own shoemaker. Every Highlander also understood the use of the hatchet, and for all ordinary purposes was his own joiner and mason; but the smith held a distinct profession, and as he could make and repair arms, was a personage of first-rate importance. Like the piper, he was an officer of the household in the Highland establishment, and generally a favourite with the chief. The arms used in the Highlands were, however, usually forged in the low country. Doune, particularly, was long remarkable for its manufacture of steel-pistols, which perhaps yet subsists. Latterly most of their fire-arms were sent from Spain or France.

The commoners, whether occasional artisans or mere peasants, had all the same character of agility and hardihood. Exposed continually to a rough climate, by the imperfect shelter afforded by their dwellings, they became indifferent to its vicissitudes; and being in the constant use of hunting and fowling, and following their cattle through morasses and over mountains, they could endure, without inconvenience, extremities of hunger and fatigue, which would destroy any other people; and hence, even in their most peaceable state, they were enured to those hardships, which, in regular armies, often destroy more than the sword. They were enthusiastic in their religion, as well as in their political principles, but were often content to take both upon trust at the recommendation, and upon the peril, of the chief. Their manners approached nearly to those of the tacksmen, being influenced by the same causes. From the self-respect, arising out of a consciousness of high descent, they displayed unusual refinement and even elegance in their ordinary address, and on important occasions possessed and exhibited a command of eloquent and figurative expressions. They were civil, brave, and hospitable; but indolent, interested, and rapacious. The arts and pretexts under which they were deprived of the produce of their labour, they combated by other arts and pretexts, by means of which they extorted from their superiors enough to support them, according to their frugal wants.

So much was the country over-peopled by the system of clanship, that in the islands, whole tribes were occasionally destroyed by famine; and even upon the continent, it was usual to bleed the cattle once a-year, that the blood thickened by oatmeal, and fried into a sort of cake, might nourish the people. But this was the last evil which the chief thought of curing. The number and military qualities of his followers were his pride and ornament, his wealth and his protection. MacDonald of Keppoch, having been called upon by an English gentleman to admire two massive silver chandeliers of uncommon beauty and workmanship, undertook a bet that when the owner should visit him in the Highlands he would show him a pair of superior value. When summoned to keep his word, he exhibited two tall Highlanders, completely equipped and armed, each holding in his right hand a blazing torch made of bog-fir. The same chief, being asked by some strangers, before whom he had placed a very handsome entertainment, what might be the rent of the estate which furnished such expenditure, answered the blunt question with equal bluntness, "I can raise five hundred men." Such was the ancient mode of computing the value of a Highland estate. "I have lived to woful days," said an Argyleshire chieftain to us in 1788; "When I was young, the only question asked concerning a man's rank, was how many men lived on his estate—then it came to be how many black cattle it could keep—but now they only ask how many sheep the lands will carry."

Such is the general view of a Highland tribe, living and governed according to the patriarchal system. But many principles, accounted fixed in theory, were occasionally departed from in practice. It might, for example, have been supposed that hereditary right was inviolably observed in a system which appeared entirely to hinge upon it. Nevertheless, in pressing circumstances, this rule was sometimes overlooked. Usurpations and revolutions also occasionally took place, as in larger principalities; and sometimes the will of the clan, excited by circumstances which displeased them in the character of the heir, set him aside upon slender grounds from the high office to which he was destined by birth. The following is an example in a clan of great note:—

When the chief of Clanronald died, his eldest son was residing, according to the Highland custom, as a foster-son in the family of Lord Lovat, chief of the Frasers. When the young man arrived at Castle Tyrim, to take possession of his estate, his attention was caught by a very profuse quantity of slaughtered cattle. He asked the meaning of this preparation, and was informed that these provisions had been made to solemnize a festival on his being first produced to his people in the character of their chief.

" I think," answered the youth, who had apparently contracted some economical ideas by residing so near the Lowlands, " I think a few hens would have made an adequate entertainment for the occasion."

This unhappy expression flew through the clan like wildfire, and excited a general sentiment of indignation.

" We will have nothing to do," they said, " with a *hen-chief*," and, dismissing the rightful heir with scorn, they called one of his brother's sons to the office and estate of the departed chief.

The Frasers, according to custom, took arms to compel the MacDonalds to do justice to their foster-child. A battle ensued—the Frasers were defeated with much slaughter, and the unlucky *hen-chief* being killed, as a miserable warning to all untimely economists, his nephew was established in the rights and power of the family. But a veil was thrown over these deviations as soon as possible; and the existing chief was always held up and maintained to be the lineal representative of the founder of the family and common father of the clan.

In like manner it was a leading principle that the clan, from the highest to the lowest, were all members of one family, bearing the same name, and connected in blood with the chief. He was expected, therefore, even in the height of his authority, to acknowledge the meanest of them as his relation, and to shake hands with him wherever they might happen to meet. There were, nevertheless, exceptions also to this rule. Small clans were sometimes totally broken up, their chiefs slain, and their independence destroyed. In this situation they became a sort of clients to some clan of greater importance, and bore to those under whom they lived very nearly the same relation which the Humsauyas, described by Mr. Elphinstone, bear to the Ooloss, or Afghan tribe, with whom they reside. Several of the most ancient of the Highland names and tribes are to be found in this state of depression.

Sometimes whole clans, without renouncing their dependence upon their own chief, subjected themselves to a tribe of predominating influence, whose name they assumed. In this cause they continued to subsist as a dependent but distinct branch of the general community; and their chief, now sunk to the rank of a chieftain, exercised his authority in subordination to that of the chief whose name he had adopted. The Campbells are said to have received numerous additions in this manner. Beside these accessions, each clan, especially when headed by a chief who stood high in the public estimation, was strengthened by individuals who came to associate themselves with the community, and who never scrupled to assume the name of the tribe. Even to this day a Highlander sometimes considers, that, upon changing his residence, a change of his name to that of his new landlord is at once a point of civility, and a means of obtaining favour. A friend of ours was shooting in the North, and as the face of the Highlander, who acted as his guide, was familiar to him, he asked if his name was not Mac-Pherson.

"No; Gordon is my name," replied the guide.

"I was shooting a few years ago at some distance from this place; you then guided me, and I remember you called yourself MacPherson."

"Yes," answerd the Highlander composedly; "but that was when I lived on the *other* side of the hill."

There yet remained another source of accession. In ancient times, the Highlanders, like the Indians, adopted prisoners of war into their tribes. Thus when the Marquis of Huntly and the Laird of Grant made a tremendous foray along Dee side, laying waste the whole dale, they carried off a great number of children whose parents they had put to death. About a year afterwards the Laird of Grant, being on a visit to Castle

Huntly, saw these children receive their food :—a kitchen trough was filled with the relics of the provisions on which the servants had dined, and at the summons of a whistle from the master cook, this mob of half naked orphans rushed in to scramble for the fragments. Shocked at the sight, Grant obtained permission to carry them into his country, where he adopted them into his own tribe, and gave them his name, which they still bear; but their descendants are distinguished from other Grants, being called "Children of the trough."

The most powerful of the Highland chiefs became in latter times frequenters of the Scottish court, and often obtained from the monarchs grants of lands and jurisdictions, which, at convenient times, they failed not to use in aid of their patriarchal authority over their own sept, and as a pretext for subjugating others. They did not, indeed, need the excuse of such authority towards the oppressed party, who lived in a state of society in which superior force necessarily constituted right.

> " For why ?—because the good old rule
>   Sufficed them ; the simple plan
>   That they should take who had the power,
>   And they should keep who can."— *Wordsworth.*

But the more prudent chiefs had now learned that there was a world beyond the mountains, and that there were laws of the kingdom which Scottish kings sometimes strove to make effectual, even among their fastnesses. And although these efforts, owing to the weakness of the government, were but transient and desultory; yet the great houses of Argyle, Huntley, Athole, and others, whose rank placed them often at court, and within the grasp of authority, found advantage in keeping *o' the windy side of the law*, and in qualifying their aggressions of their Highland neighbours by such plausible forms as might pass current in case of enquiry at the seat of government. Nothing was more hateful to their ruder neighbours than claims of this kind, which they neither understood nor acknowledged. The mode in which the rights of jurisdiction obtained by the higher families were exercised, had little tendency to reconcile the less powerful chiefs to what they considered as legalized modes of oppression.

"Take care of yourselves in Sutherland," said an old Highlander as he communicated the alarming news which he had just learned, "the *law* is come as far as Tain."

Accordingly, the execution of the laws, to the last, was resisted in the Highlands: nor was the authority of the magistrates respected, nor durst any inferior officer of the law execute his duty. The traces of this state of manners were long visible: and so late as thirty years since, and within twenty miles of Stirling Castle, it was found necessary to obtain a military escort, to protect the officer who was to serve a civil process giving a Highland tenant warning to remove.

CHAPTER V.

The Great Ruling Families—Historical Account of the Highlands—
King James I.—The Lords of the Isles—Feuds in the Clan Colla
—Numerous clans and their history and location—Early Statutes
relating to Highland feuds—The Clan MacGregor—Their remarkable History and Career—Tragic occurrences.

THIS state of disorder cannot be imputed to the
neglect of the Scottish parliament, who frequently
exercised their sagacity in framing laws for the regula-
tions of the Highlands and Borders: the high grounds
of which last were, until the union of the crowns, in
the same, or in a more lawless condition than the Highlands themselves. But previously to any notice of these
laws, it will be necessary to give a brief retrospect of
the state of the Highlands before they were so united
with the rest of the kingdom as to be proper subjects
for its legislature. We have already observed that, in
former times, the Highland chiefs paid allegiance to
princes of their own, altogether distinct from the King
of Scotland, with whom they were sometimes at war,
sometimes at peace, or, at the utmost, acknowledged
only a slight and nominal dependence upon him;—
this was that powerful dynasty of the Lords of the
Isles, who flourished, from a dark and remote period,
down to the reign of James V. Their authority extended over all the western islands, from Islay northward, over Kintyre, Knapdale, and the western parts
of Inverness-shire; and they exercised the influence of
powerful allies, if not of lords paramount, over the

M'Dougals, Lords of Lorn.   Their claim to the earldom
of Ross often laid that northern county at their disposal;
and their supremacy was disputed in that district by
the Earls of Sutherland alone.   These districts make
up the bulk of the Highlands.

The rest was swayed by the Strathbogies, Earls of
Athol, who had under their authority, Athole, Strathbogie, and Lochaber; by the Cumings, in Badenoch;
by the Earls of Mar, in the Highlands of Aberdeenshire; the Earl of Lennox, in Dumbartonshire; and the
Knight of Lochowe, in Argyleshire.   Many of the Highland lords, having taken part against Bruce in his
struggles for the crown, were involved in ruin by his
success : among those were the families of Cuming of
Strathbogie, and of MacDougal, whose power passed
over to the Stuarts, Campbells, Gordons, Murrays, and
other favourers of the Bruce interests, to whom were
granted their forfeited domains.   It was said of the
English who settled in Ireland, that they became *ipsis
Hibernis Hiberniores;* and therefore we cannot be surprised that the new Highland lords conformed themselves to the fashion of their new subjects, and assumed
the part and character of chiefs, which had so much to
flatter ambition and the love of power.   But though
these changes of possession contributed greatly to
limit the power of the Lords of the Isles, it remained
sufficiently exorbitant to alarm and disturb the rest of
Scotland; and it was not until the battle of the Harlaw, fought in 1410, in which the power of that insular

kingdom received a severe check, that it could be considered as an actual dependence of the Scottish crown.

Upon the accession of James I. the power of the northern chiefs was somewhat restricted, and many royal castles, particularly that of Inverness, were rebuilt and garrisoned. The King himself took a journey to the Highlands ; and, having had his education in England, was not a little surprised at the state of anarchy which pervaded this part of his dominions. He learned that, within a few miles of his present residence, were heads of a banditti, who had each from one to two thousand men at their call; who lived entirely by plunder, and acknowledged no limit of their actions but their own will. James I. was an active and intelligent monarch, and so far exerted himself as to compel the Lord of the Isles to submission, and utterly to destroy a large force of Highlanders and Islesmen who rose in his favour, under the leading of his cousin, Donald Balloch. Balloch himself was put to death by an Irish chief, to whom he had fled for protection, and three hundred of his followers were condemned to the gibbet.

During the troubles occasioned by the rebellion of the Douglasses, the Lords of the Isles once more gained ground. But about the year 1476, the King was able to reduce them again to nominal subjection, and what was more material, to diminish their actual power, by the resumption of the earldom of Ross, with the large districts of Knapdale and Kintyre, which, in

a great measure, excluded the Lords of the Isles from
interference with the continent.   The uncertainty of
Highland succession had already raised up rivals to
the Lords of the Isles, in the pretensions of their kinsmen; and about the reign of James V., the last Mac-
Donald who asssumed that title died without male
heirs; and a family whose power had so long rivalled
and excelled that of the Kings of Scotland, in the
northern part of their dominions, became extinct as a
dynasty.

The main stock of the Lords of the Isles being thus
decayed, there arose many shoots from the trunk. But
these branches of *Clan Colla*, for such is the general
name of that powerful sept, prevented each other's
growth by mutual rivalry; and though strong and
powerful, neither approached in consequence nor
strength to the parent tree.   These were the families
of Slate, Clanronald, Glengarry, Keppoch, Ardnamurchan, Glencoe, and Largo, all, especially those
first named, independent tribes of great importance
and consequence.   But debates amongst themselves
prevented the name of MacDonald from ever attaining
its original pitch of power.   Their feuds were rendered
more bitter by their propinquity, and, even in the last
days of chieftainship, tended to weaken the cause
which most of them had espoused.   After the battle of
Falkirk, in 1746, the musket of a MacDonald, of the
tribe of Clanronald, chanced unhappily to go off while
he was cleaning it, and killed a hopeful young gentle-

man, a son of Glengarry, who commanded the men of his father's clan. So sacred was the claim of blood for blood, that the execution of the poor fellow through whose negligence this mischance had happened was judged indispensable by the council of chiefs. The accident was of the worst consequence to the Chevalier's cause both ways; for most of the Glengarry men went home, disheartened by the fate of their leader, and released from the restraint of his authority : and many of Clanronald's people did the same, from a natural disgust at the severity exercised on their clansman for an involuntary fault.

Besides these leading branches, there were many tribes distinguished by other patronymics, who claimed their descent from the same stock ; but who remained separate and independent. Among these, if we mistake not (for heaven forbid we should speak with unbecoming confidence!) are the MacAlisters, MacKeans, MacNabs,* MacIntyres, MacKeachans, MacKechnies, and MacAphies—a list which involuntarily reminds us of the sonorous names of the Brazilian tribes, Tupinikins, Tupigais, Tupinayes, and Tupinambas. But exclusive of these descendants of MacDonald, and, indeed, in a degree of public importance far superior to many of them, were the clans whose chiefs had held offices of trust under the Lords of the Isles, and who now attained a formidable independence, augmented by the

* In some genealogies the MacNabs are claimed by the MacAlpines and MacGregors as descended from the same root with them.

shares which they had been able to secure in the wreck of the principal family.

Such were the MacLeans, long lieutenants of the Lords of the Isles; the MacKenzies, who had already obtained many grants from regal favour; the Camerons, the MacNeils, the MacIntoshes, and many other clans which had hitherto been subjected to the regal tribe of Clan Colla. The Kings of Scotland favoured this division of power, upon the grand political maxim of dividing in order to command; but although the separation of the tribes was very complete, it by no means appears that the authority of the sovereign was increased in proportion. It was true, indeed, that, being no longer under one common head, the Highland clans were not so capable of disturbing the general peace of the kingdom : but when political circumstances concurred to unite any number of chiefs in a common cause, the mountain eruption broke out with as much violence as under the Lords of the Isles. Meanwhile, the internal feuds of the tribes became, if possible, more deadly than before; and though those who were of Lowland origin, and connected with the crown, gradually gained ground upon the others, it was not without the most desperate struggles.

In the preamble of an act of James IV. it is declared that for want of justice-airs, justices, and sheriffs, the Islesmen and the Highlanders had almost become savage ; and some steps are taken for establishing legal jurisdictions among them. But the evil was too powerful for the remedy. In the vigorous reign of James V. further measures were adopted—the King in person undertook a voyage around the northern part of Britain, and impressed the inhabitants of these wild isles and mountains with some sense of the existence of a power paramount to that of their chiefs. But this also soon passed away, and the civil wars of Queen Mary's time set every independent chief at liberty to work his own pleasure, under pretext of espousing one or other of the contending factions.

A statute, in the year 1581, declares "that one great cause of the oppressions and cruelties daily practised in the realm is, that clans of thieves were associated together by a common surname, not subject to any landlord (that is, feudal superior), nor amenable to the common laws of justice: and holding inveterate and deadly feud against all true men who had been concerned in repressing by violence, any of their enormities;" it therefore enacts, that all men sustaining injury by them should be at liberty to make reprisals, not only on the individual perpetrators, but also to slay or arrest any person whatever, being of the same clan with those from which they received the injury. This tended only to give a legal and colourable pretext for private wars and deadly feuds, already too prevalent; another regulation therefore, was adopted in the year 1587.

This remarkable statute, after setting forth that "the inhabitants of the Borders, Highlands, and Isles, delighted in all mischiefs, taking advantage of each intestine state-commotion which relaxed the hands of ordinary justice, most unnaturally and cruelly to waste, harry, slay, and destroy their own neighbours and native country-people," proceeds to promulgate a roll of their captains, chiefs, and chieftains, as well of the principal branches of each tribe as of the tribe in general; and to declare that these leaders should be obliged to find security, rendering themselves personally responsible for whatever damage should be committed by their clansmen or dependents. This, while it seemed to legalize the authority of the chiefs, hitherto unacknow-ledged by any positive statute, had, after the union of the crowns, very great influence upon the Borders, and might also have produced some good consequences on the Highlands, had it been as strictly administered. One effect, however, was, that several clans which, by the encroachment of their neighbours, or the miscarriage of their own schemes of ambition, had been driven out of the lands, were in no condition to find the security required by law, and were, therefore, denounced as outlaws and broken men. The most remarkable of these was the clan Gregor, or MacGregors, of which most of our readers must have heard.

This family, or sept, is of genuine Celtic origin, great antiquity, and in Churchhill's phrase,

————————————" doubtless springs
From great and glorious, but forgotten kings."

They were once possessed of Glenurchy, of the castle

at the head of Lochowe, of Glendochart, Glenlyon,
Finlarig, Balloch, now called Taymouth, and of the
greater part of Breadalbane. From these territories
they were gradually expelled by the increasing strength
of the Campbells, who, taking advantage of a bloody
feud between the MacGregors and MacNabs, obtained
letters of fire and sword against the former, and about
the reign of James III. and IV. dispossessed them of
much of their property. The celebrated MacGregor a
Rua, Rua, the heir-male of the chief, and a very gallant
young man, was surprised and slain by Colin Campbell,
the knight of Lochowe, and with him fell the fortunes
of his family. From this time, the few lands which
remained in their possession being utterly inadequate
to maintain so numerous a clan, the MacGregors became
desperate, wild and lawless, supporting themselves
either by actual depredation, or by the money which
they levied as the price of their forbearance, and retali-
ating upon the more powerful clans, as well as upon the
Lowlands, the severity with which they were frequently
pursued and slaughtered. A single trait of their history
will show what was the ferocity of feud among the
Scottish clans.

The remaining settlements of the MacGregor tribe
were chiefly in Balquhidder, around Loch Katrine, and
as far as the borders of Loch Lomond. Even these
lands they did not possess in property, but by some
transaction with the family of Buchanan, who were the
real landholders; but the terrors of the MacGregors

extended far and wide, for they were at feud with
almost all their neighbours.

In the year 1589, a party of MacGregors, belonging
to a tribe called *Clan Düil a Cheach, i.e.* the Children
of Dugald of the Mist (an appropriate term for such a
character), met with John Drummond of Drummondernoch, a ranger of the royal forest of Glenartney, as
he was seeking venison for the King's use. It chanced
that Drummondernoch had, in his capacity of steward-
depute, or provincial magistrate, of Strathearn, tried
and executed two or three of these MacGregors for
depredations committed on his chief Lord Drummond's
lands. The Children of the Mist seized the opportunity
of vengeance, slew the unfortunate huntsman, and cut
off his head : they then went to the house of Stuart of
Ardvoirlich, whose wife was a sister of the murdered
Drummondernoch. The laird was absent, but the lady
received the unbidden, and probably unwelcome guests
with hospitality, and, according to the Highland custom
and phrase, placed before them bread and cheese till
better food could be made ready.

She left the room to superintend the preparations,
and when she returned, beheld, displayed upon the
table, the ghastly head of her brother, with a morsel of
bread and cheese in its mouth. The terrified lady
rushed out of the house with a fearful shriek, and could
not be found, though her distracted husband caused all
the woods and wildernesses around to be diligently
searched. To augment the misery of Ardvoirlich, his

unfortunate wife was with child when she disappeared. She did not, however, perish. It was the harvest season, and in the woods and moors the maniac wanderer probably found berries, and other substances capable of sustaining life; though the vulgar, fond of the marvellous, suppose that the wild-deer had pity on her misery and submitted to be milked by her. At length some train of former ideas and habits began to revive in her mind. She had formerly been very attentive to her domestic duties, and used commonly to oversee the milking of the cows—and now the women employed in that office, in the remote upland grazings, observed with terror, that they were regularly watched, during the milking, by an emaciated miser- able-looking female figure, who appeared from among the bushes, but retired with great swiftness when any one approached her.

The story was told to Ardvoirlich, who, conjecturing the truth, took measures for intercepting and recovering the unfortunate fugitive. She regained her senses after the birth of her child; but it was remarkable that the son whom she bore seemed affected by the con- sequence of her terror. He was of great strength, but of violent passions, under the influence of which he killed his friend and commander, Lord Kilpont, in a manner which the reader will find detailed in Wishart's *Memoirs of Montrose.*

The tragedy of Drummondernoch did not conclude with the effects of the murder on the Lady Ardvoirlich.

The clan of the MacGregors being convoked in the church of Balquhidder, upon the Sunday after the act, the bloody head was produced on the altar, when each clansman avowed the murder to have been perpetrated by his own consent, and laying successively his hands on the scalp, swore to protect and defend the authors of the deed ;—" in ethnic and barbarous manner," says an order of the lords of the privy council, dated 4th February 1589, " in most proud contempt of our sovereign lord and his authority and in evil example to other wicked *limmers* to do the like, if this shall be suffered to remain unpunished." Then follows a commission—" to seek for and pursue Alaster MacGregor, of Glenstrae, and all others of his name, with fire and sword."

We have seen a letter upon this subject, from Patrick Lord Drummond, who was naturally most anxious to revenge his kinsman's death, to the Earl of Montrose, appointing a day in which the one shall be " at the bottom of the valley of Balquhidder with his forces, and advance upward, and the other with his powers shall occupy the higher outlet, and move downwards for the express purpose of taking *sweet revenge* for the death of their cousin." Ardvoirlich assisted them with a party, and it is said they killed thirty-seven of the clan of Dugald of the Mist upon the single farm of Invernenty. The death of Drummondernoch is the subject of a beautiful poem by Alexander Boswell, of Auchinleck, entitled " Clan-

Alpine's Vow." The King himself entered keenly into the success of the feud, as appears from a letter to the Laird of M'Intosh still preserved in Sir Æneas M'Intosh's charter-chest at Moyhall. The letter is as follows: and it will show that the taste for heads was not confined to the Children of the Mist, since the King requests one to be sent to him.

Right traist Freynd, We greet you hairtlie well. Having heard be report of the laite preeife given be you, of your willing disposition to our service, in prosequiteing of that wicked race of M'Gregor, we haife thought meit hereby to signifie unto you, that we accompt the same as maist acceptable pleasure and service done unto us, and will not omitt to regard the same as it deserves; and because we ar to give you out of our aein mouthe sum furder directionn thair anent,—it is our will, that upon the sight hereof ye repaire hither in all haist, and at yr arriving we sall impairt or full mynde, and heir wt all we haif thought expedient, that ye, befoir yor arriving hither, sall caus execut to the death Duncane M'Can Caim, latelie tane be you in yor last *(expedition)* agains the clan Gregor, and caus his heid to be transportit hither, to the effect the same may be affixt in sum public place, to the terror of other malefactors, and so comitt you to God. From Haly rud hous, the penult day of *
in the year 1596.   (Signed)   JAMES R.

On the back—Lre be King James to M'Intosh about the year 1596.

The "revenge" was doubtless ample; but Alaster

* The month was interlined and illegible.

MacGregor's power was so little impaired, that, in 1602, he was able to sustain the desperate battle of Glenfruin, in which he defeated the Laird of Luss, and almost extirpated the name of Colquhoun. For this battle and the outrages which preceded and followed it, the clan were formally outlawed by act of Parliament, and it was made an offence equal to felony, to take or bear that proscribed surname: thus held up as a prey to destruction, they were attacked on all sides, pursued with blood-hounds, and when seized, put to death without even the formalities of a trial. The chief himself, Alaster of Glenstrae, surrendered with eighteen of his most faithful followers to the Earl of Argyle, on condition that he should conduct him safe out of Scotland. But, says old Birrel, the Earl kept a Highlander's promise, for he sent him under a guard as far as Berwick, but with instructions not to set him at liberty. So after this airing upon English ground for the acquittal of Argyle's word, the unfortunate chief was brought back to Edinburgh, and hanged at the cross of that city, a man's height higher than his companions, who were executed at the same time. Yet such was the vivifying principle inherent in clanship, that the MacGregors, though proscribed and persecuted, under the authority of repeated statutes, continued to exist as a numerous and separate clan, until their name was restored to them in our own days.

CHAPTER VI.

The Campbells in the West Highlands—Conflicts between Highlanders and Lowlanders—The wars of Montrose—Cromwell and the Highlanders—The Highlanders at the Restoration—The MacDonalds of Keppoch and the MacIntoshs—The House of Hanover and the Highlanders.

THE Earl of Argyle had now acquired very great authority in the West Highlands and Isles, which he augmented by suppressing some troubles which arose among the MacDonalds; in consideration of which, his family got a grant of the district of Kintyre. But excepting that this great family in the west, and those of Huntley and Athole in the north, had succeeded both to direct authority over many clans, and to great influence over others, the state of the Highlands remained the same in Charles First's as in his father's time.

With the civil wars the Highlanders assumed a new and more distinguished character; and for the first time in our history showed a marked and distinguished superiority in the use of arms over their Lowland fellow-subjects. The cause of this is abundantly obvious. In former times, when the Highlanders descended from their mountains, they encountered in the Lowlands, a race of men as hardy, brave, and skilful in the use of weapons as themselves, and far superior to them in arms and military discipline. In the battle of Harlaw, Donald of the Isles, with the largest army that ever left the Highlands, was checked by an inferior number of Lowlanders; and in the fields of Corichie, Glenlivat, and others, the Highlanders were routed with great loss, by fewer but better appointed numbers of their Lowland countrymen.

But the lapse of more than half a century had placed the Lowlanders in a different situation. During the reign of Charles I. they had remained quiet under the protection of the laws; neither doing nor suffering violence; and the martial spirit had much decayed among them. The success, therefore, of the Highlanders in Montrose's wars is not wonderful. They were not only bred to arms and active exercises from their infancies, but were in a manner regimented under their several chiefs and tacksmen ; so that, being always in order for war, they wanted but a general and a cause. Their advantage in encountering the tumultary forces of the covenanting Lowlanders, who had detached to England all their regular troops, and brought to the field only a disorderly militia, had all the success which could have been anticipated. It will be best accounted for by the expressions of a contemporary, the Rev. Robert Baillie, who writes to his correspondent, Mr. William Spang, minister of Campvere, in Zealand, 25th April, 1645.

" The country forces of Fife and Stratherne were three to one—well armed—had horse and cannon;— but the treachery of Kilpont, and especially Sir John Drummond, together with Elcho's rashness, delivered all that tumultous people and their arms into the enemy's hands without a stroke. A great number of burgesses were killed;—twenty-five householders in St.

Andrew's only ;—*many were bursten in the flight, and died without stroke.*" It is obvious that men who died of the exertion of running away, could be no match, either in onset or retreat, for the hardy, agile, and long-breathed Highlanders.   After gaining many battles, however, and overrunning all Scotland, Montrose was finally defeated by a body of regular forces commanded by David Lesley.   But from the time of his wars the Highlanders asserted and maintained, in all the civil dissensions of Scotland, a marked and decided superiority over their Lowland fellow-subjects, which tended not a little to exalt their opinion of their own import-ance, and to render them tenacious of the customs and usages of their country.   The same period, however, which witnessed their first brilliant display of victories beyond the bounds of their own mountains, also saw the Highland clans receive, even within their strongest fastnesses, a chastisement which the hands of their own monarchs had never been powerful enough to inflict.

The stern policy of Cromwell established garrisons at Inverness, Inverlochy, and other places in the High-lands—he set on foot movable columns, who constantly patrolled the country, and became acquainted with its most hidden recesses ;—the castles of the chiefs were destroyed, the woods that sheltered them were cut down, and, finally, in spite of the valour of the clans, and the enthusiasm of their chiefs, he compelled them to sur-render their arms, and to give pledges of their peace-able conduct.   And it is generally allowed that, as the

Highlands had never been in such quiet subjection until this period, so their neighbours never enjoyed such an interval of rest from their incursions until after the year 1745. The rigorous discipline of Cromwell was equally successful in crushing the spirit of chivalry among the rude mountain-chiefs as among the cavaliers of England ; and so strong was the impression which his arms made on their imagination, that, in 1726, an aged Highland laird told Mr. Burt, that Oliver's colours were so strongly fixed in his memory, that he still thought he saw them spread out by the wind, and bearing the word EMANUEL upon them, in very large golden characters.*

Upon the Restoration, the Stuarts, who owed so much to the Highland clans, for what they had done and suffered in the royal cause, under Montrose, Glencairn and Middleton, rewarded the chiefs by relaxing the discipline under which Cromwell had placed them. The forts established at Inverness, and elsewhere, for bridling the mountaineers, were dismantled or abandoned. The Marquis of Argyle (in Highland phrase Gillespie Gruomach) had acquired a prodigious ascendancy in the Western Highlands and Isles during the civil wars, and received from Parliament many large grants both of lands and jurisdiction. It is well known by what means and for what causes Charles II. and his brother prosecuted the ruin of this nobleman and his son, in

* Letters from the North of Scotland.—Letter XI.

consequence of which, the MacDonalds, MacLeans, and other clans, who had been overpowered by the weight of the marquis's authority, were restored to independence.

The Duke of York, during his residence at Edinburgh, had frequent opportunities of becoming acquainted with the principal northern chieftains, whose stately *fierté* well suited his own reserved and haughty temper : they were, besides, either Catholics, or bigoted to the prelatic establishment; and, in either case, were deemed fit persons to countenance, in opposition to the Presbyterian interest, so odious to the reigning family. The laws against their excesses were therefore greatly relaxed; and it was even thought politic to employ the clans in overawing the western shires, where the prohibited conventicles of the Presbyterians were most numerous. Six thousand Highlanders were invited from their mountains to pillage these devoted counties; a task which they performed with the rapacity of an indigent people attracted by objects of luxury to which they were strangers, but with less cruelty than had perhaps been expected from them. In the meanwhile, encouraged by these marks of favour and indulgence, they had again established their own exemptions from the general law of Scotland, both in civil and criminal concerns, as will appear from the curious case of MacDonald of Keppoch.

This chief and the laird of Macintosh had long disputed a territory called Glenroy, in the central High-

lands. MacIntosh had obtained a crown charter, com-
prehending a grant of these lands. Keppoch, disdain-
ing, as he said, to *hold his lands in a sheepskin*, took
forcible possession of Glenroy, and there maintained
himself. MacIntosh, in 1687, with the assistance of a
body of regular forces, commanded by MacKenzie of
Suddy, summoned his clan, and marched against
Keppoch, but received a severe defeat at Milroy, where
Suddy was slain, he himself made prisoner, and compelled to renounce his right to the lands in dispute. A
strong body of military was next marched into the
Highlands to revenge this insult, and under the
authority of letters of fire and sword, Keppoch's lands
were laid waste with great severity.* Yet this did not
break the strength, or diminish the spirit of Keppoch,
for in 1689 he was able to lay siege to Inverness; and,
what is still more extraordinary, the severe usage
which he had received did not diminish his zeal for the
Stuart family, for he was the first to join the standard
which the Viscount of Dundee raised against King
William.

Dundee, a man at once of genius and of military experience, knew how to avail himself of the enthusiastic
energy of a Highland army, and to conciliate and
direct the discordant councils of their independent
chiefs. He fell in the battle of Killiecrankie, one of the
greatest victories ever gained by an Highland army;

* See Crichton's *Memoirs* in Swift's works: Captain Crichton was
himself employed on this occasion.

and those who succeeded in the command, being men of routine, and of limited views, the war dwindled away into a succession of inroads and skirmishes, in the course of which the bordering Highlanders plundered the low country so severely, that in many districts the year of the *hership* (plunder) was long afterwards mentioned as an era. King William, just arrived at the possession of a crown which seemed still precarious, and having his attention engaged by the continental war, and that of Ireland, thought it best to purchase peace in this remote corner of his new kingdom, and the Earl of Bredalbane was intrusted with £20,000 sterling, to be distributed among the Highland chiefs. Bredalbane was artful, daring, and rapacious. Some chiefs he gratified with a share of the money; others with good words; others he kept quiet by threats; and it has always been supposed that the atrocity well known by the name of the massacre of Glencoe, was devised and executed to gratify at once an ancient quarrel, to silence an intractable chief, who had become clamorous about the division of the peace-offering, and to serve as a measure of intimidation to all others. It is said that when Bredalbane was required by the English minister to account for the sum of money put into his hands for the above purpose, he returned this laconic answer—

"My Lord, the money is spent—the Highlands are quiet—and this is the only way of accounting among friends."

This termination of a war, by a subsidy grant to the insurgents, was by no means calculated to lower that idea of their own consequence, which the Highland chiefs most readily entertained at all times. Each set about augmenting his followers by every means in his power, regarding military strength as the road to wealth and importance in the national convulsions which seemed approaching.

Contrary, however, to what might have been expected, the crisis of the accession of the Hanover family did not at first make a strong impression on the Highland chiefs. After much consultation among themselves, an address was drawn up to congratulate George I. on his accession to the throne, and to implore his favour. We give this curious document. We are ignorant whether it has ever appeared in any collection of state papers. Ours is given to us as copied from a manuscript of the period; and though this remarkable paper is unnoticed in history, we believe it to be genuine. It is entitled—

" *Address of one hundred and two Chief Heritors and Heads of Clans in the Highlands of Scotland, to King George the First, on his Accession to the Throne, which by Court Intrigue was prevented from being delivered to his Majesty: the consequence was, their joining in the Rebellion in the year* 1715.

" May it please your Majesty,

" We of the chief heritors and others, in the Highlands of Scotland, under subscribing, beg leave to express the joy of our hearts at your Majesty's happy accession to the crown of Great Britain. Your Majesty has the blood of our ancient monarchs in your veins and in your family; may that royal race ever continue to reign over us! Your Majesty's princely virtues, and the happy prospect we have in your royal family of an uninterrupted succession of kings to sway the British sceptre, must extinguish those divisions and contests which in former times too much prevailed, and unite all who have the happiness to live under your Majesty into a firm obedience and loyalty to your Majesty's person, family, and government; and as our predecessors have for many ages had the honour to distinguish themselves by their loyalty, so we do most humbly assure your Majesty, that we will reckon it our honour steadfastly to adhere to you, and with our lives and fortunes to support your crown and dignity against all oppressors. Pardon us, great Sir, to implore your royal protection against any who labour to misrepresent us, and who rather use their endeavours to create misunderstandings than to engage the hearts of subjects to that loyalty and cheerful obedience which we owe, and are happy to testify towards your Majesty. Under so excellent a king, we are persuaded that we, and all our other peaceable and faithful subjects, shall enjoy their just rights and liberties, and that our enemies shall not be able to hurt us with your Majesty, for whose royal favour we presume humbly to hope, as our forefathers were honoured with that of your Majesty's ancestors. Our mountains, though undervalued by some, are nevertheless acknowledged to have at all times been fruitful in providing hardy and gallant men, and such, we hope, shall never be wanting amongst us, who shall be ready to undergo all

dangers in defence of your Majesty, and your royal
posterity's only rightful title to the crown of Great
Britain.   Our behaviour shall always witness for us,
that with unalterable firmness and zeal we are,

  "May it please your Majesty,

        "Your Majesty's most loyal, most obedient

              "And most dutiful subjects and servants,

                    "ALEX. MACDONALD, of Glengarry,
                    "MACINTOSH, of that Ilk,
                    "J. CAMERON, of Lochiele,
                    "J. STEWART, of Ardsheall,
                    "NORMAN MACLEOD, of Drynach,"
                          &c. &c.

It is said to have been delivered to Archibald Duke
of Argyle, to be presented by him to the new sovereign:
but that nobleman, being a politician as well as a soldier, is alleged to have seen more prospect of personal
aggrandisement in an insurrection, which would render
his services indispensable, than in a peaceful submission of the Highlands to the House of Hanover.   Accordingly, the Earl of Marr came over to Scotland;
the standard of the Chevalier St. George was raised;
and almost all the Highland chiefs of name and emin-
ence assembled their forces at Perth.   But Marr, by
whom they were commanded, was better fitted for the
intrigues of a court, than for leading an army and
directing a campaign; and a force of Highlanders, the
greatest ever assembled, and which, under Montrose,
Dundee, or even Charles Edward, would have made
itself master of all Scotland, was (with the exception

of the forlorn hope under Mackintosh of Borlum, which shared the fate of the Northumbrian insurgents) completely neutralized, and pent up within the friths of Clyde and Forth, by the Duke of Argyle at the head of a force not exceeding two or three thousand men.

The indecisive battle of Sheriffmuir only served to show the incapacity of the Jacobite general, and the valour of the troops he commanded. It was upon this memorable day that young Clanronald fell, leading on the Highlanders of the right wing. His death dispirited the assailants, who began to waver. But Glengarry, chief of a rival branch of the Clan Colla, started from the ranks, and waving his bonnet round his head, cried out:

" To-day for revenge, and to-morrow for mourning!"

" The Highlanders received a new impulse from his words, and, charging with redoubled fury, bore down all before them. But their left wing was less fortunate, being completely routed, and pushed as far as the river Allan, two miles from the field of battle. Both parties retreated after this doubtful action, the Highlanders to Perth, the Duke of Argyll to Stirling: but the ultimate advantage rested with the former.

CHAPTER VII.

Lord President Forbes—The Story of Lord Lovat's Life—The Tragic Story of his Marriage—Lord Lovat's Intrigues—Lord President Forbes' Exertions on behalf of his Countrymen.

AT this period of Highland history, Duncan Forbes,

afterwards President of the Court of Session, and whose original papers and correspondence are here given to the world, made a considerable figure in public affairs. He was a younger son of the family of Culloden, which had a considerable estate in the neighbourhood of Inverness, and was thus connected by blood and friendship with almost all the respectable families in that district, and with many of the Highland chiefs. Mr. Forbes was educated to the law, in which he was early distinguished, not more by eloquence than by sound sense and depth of knowledge. At the time of the insurrection in 1715, his elder brother, John Forbes, of Culloden, as well as himself, engaged with heart and hand in the service of the government, to which they were enabled to render important services, partly through their own influence and exertions, partly by means of a chief, whose history forms a strange illustration of the effect of power and ambition upon a mind naturally shrewd, crafty and resolute, but wild, tameless, and unprincipled: this was the celebrated Simon Fraser, of Lovat, of whose previous history we must give the outlines.

Simon was the son of Thomas Fraser of Beaufort, next male heir to the house of Lovat after the death of Hugh Lord Lovat, without issue male. Being regarded as the heir apparent of the chieftainship as well as of the estate of Lovat, he attempted to unite by marriage his own claim with that of the eldest daughter of the deceased Lord Hugh. The dowager Lady Lovat was

a daughter of the Marquis of Athole; and that powerful family was therefore induced to take great interest
in disposing of the young lady in marriage. Various
quarrels, during the time that Simon of Beaufort held
a commission in his regiment, had made him particularly unacceptable to the Marquis of Athole and his
family, who viewed his assuming the title of Master of
Lovat, and proposing himself as a husband for their
kinswoman, with a very evil eye: they therefore removed the young lady to Dunkeld, and set on foot a
match between her and Lord Saltoun, a Lowland
family bearing the name of Fraser.

When Lord Saltoun, accompanied by Athole's
brother, Lord Mungo Murray, and other connexions of
the family, entered upon the territories of the Frasers,
with the purpose of paying his respects to the mother
of his intended bride, they were surprised, seized, and
disarmed, by Simon, to whom the greater part of the
clan adhered, as representing his father, their true
chief. Having gained this advantage, he attempted to
improve it by an act of depravity, which can hardly be
accounted for, except by irregularity of intellect, and
an eager desire to put a deep dishonour and mortal
displeasure upon the family of Athole. As the heiress,
the original object of his suit, made no part of his
prisoners, but remained secure in the castle of Dunkeld,
he abandoned all thoughts of that alliance, and formed
the strange and apparently sudden resolution of marrying her mother, the Dowager Lady Lovat.

Having raised a gallows on the green before Castle-Downie, where she then resided, to intimidate all who might protect the object of his violence,—a lady advanced in life, and whose person is said to have been as little inviting as her character was respectable—he went through the mock ceremony of a wedding, and had her dress cut from her person with a dirk, and subjected her to the last extremity of brutal violence, while the pipes played in the next apartment to drown her screams. This outrage Lovat has positively denied, in the Memoirs of his own Life, where he terms the accusation a chimera raised up to blacken his character: but we shall soon see reason to believe that his assertions were not always squared by matter of fact. Besides, he denies the marriage as well as the force with which it was perpetrated, and declares that he never even approached her person; assigning many reasons why she could neither be an object to him of desire nor of ambition.* Now, in a letter from his father to the Earl of Argyle, subscribed by himself and other gentleman of his clan, he says:

" Also they'll have my son and complices guilty of a rape, though *his wife was married to him by a minister*, and they have always lived since as man and wife." †

It may be more difficult to conceive how Lovat, blackened with such an unmanly crime, was at any

* Memoirs of the Life of Simon Lord Lovat. London, 1797. 8vo., p. 60.

† Carstairs' State Papers, p. 434.

time afterwards considered as fit society for men of
honour, and particularly how he could become the
friend of such a man as Duncan Forbes.   This might
partly arise from the practice in the Highlands.   Even
in ordinary cases, the bride was expected to affect some
reluctance; and the greater or less degree of violence
did not, in these wild times, appear a matter of much
consequence.   The Scottish law-books are crowded
with instances of this sort of *raptus*, or, as it is called in
their law, "*forcible abduction of women.*"   The inference
seems to be, that, in some circumstances, no absolute
infamy was attached even to those acts of violence,
from which it seems impossible to divide it : and we remember a woman on the banks of Loch Lomond, herself the daughter of such a marriage, who repelled,
with great contempt, the idea of its being a real
grievance on the bride, and said that, in her time, the
happiest matches were always so made.   These particulars are only quoted to mark public opinion; but it
may be a better answer that, as Duncan Forbes was
not so squeamish as to quarrel with the society of
Colonel Charteris, there is less wonder that he endured
that of Lovat.

He had defended Charteris in a trial for a rape, and
obtained from his gratitude the gratuitous use of a little
villa near Musselburgh, called Stoney-hill.   We ought
to add that, in spite of poets and satirists, or whatever
might be Charteris's general character, the charge of
rape was an atrocious attempt to levy money from him

by terror. Still there is something ludicrous in the coincidence, that two special friends of so respectable a man should have both been *in trouble* on so infamous an accusation.

In 1698, Simon Fraser was summoned to answer before the Privy Council, for the crimes of unlawfully assembling the lieges in arms, and for the violence offered to the Lady Dowager Lovat. Against the first (which was no great crime in a Highland chief), he offered no defence; but the Earl of Argyle stated, that he was willing to refer the circumstances of the marriage to his wife's oath. He did not, however, appear; and a variety of witnesses being examined, tending to establish the crime in its fullest extent, sentence of outlawry went forth against the delinquent. He skulked for some time in the Highlands, and displayed both address and courage in defeating many attempts made by the Athole men to seize his person; but at length he was compelled to fly to the continent. Meanwhile the young heiress, at whose hand he had originally aimed, was wedded to Alexander Mackenzie, son of one of the Judges of Session, called Lord Prestonhall, who assumed, upon this marriage, the title of Fraserdale.

The earnest solicitations of the Duke of Argyle (hereditary enemy to the family of Athole) had, through the medium of Mr. Carstairs, obtained from King William a remission of the crime of high treason, of which Simon Fraser had been declared guilty; but the rape being one of a more private and atrocious complexion, his pardon did not extend to it; and thus he still remained an exile from Scotland. His daring and intriguing spirit carried him now to the court of Saint Germain's, where he proposed a plan of invasion, if men and money could be furnished by the French king, and pledged himself that the invading forces should be joined by the principal chiefs of the Highlands, with ten thousand men. Louis did not approve of the personal security on which he was required to hazard his subjects and treasures, although Fraser, to give more weight to it, had publicly adopted the Catholic religion.

He was sent over, however, to intrigue in Scotland, with the friends of the exiled family, accompanied by Captain James Murray, who was to act as a spy, or check, upon him. But finding a slackness in the Tory party, to whom he applied himself, for most of them were contented with the government of Queen Anne, now upon the throne, Fraser began to try what could be gained on the other side. He opened, accordingly, an intercourse with Queensberry and Leven, heads of the opposite party, who instantly saw the advantage they might derive from involving the Dukes of Hamilton, Athole, and other rivals of their power, in a Jacobitical plot; and that it might ripen into something more decisive, they granted a passport for Fraser to return to France, under a feigned name. But this emissary's purposes of hatching up a conspiracy, which he might forward or betray, as best suited his interest, proved too weighty for his means of executing them. The Tory party got scent of his intrigues with Queensberry and Leven; and as there was every prospect of his hand-grenade exploding while it was yet in his grasp, he fled, in great haste, to France, where he was immediately committed to the state prison of Angoulême. He regained his liberty, but, distrusted as he now was on all sides, he had no opportunity to engage in any new intrigues, until the memorable year 1715.

At the time when all the Jacobite clans were in arms, and drawn towards the midland counties, it appeared to the Duke of Argyle and to Mr. Forbes of Culloden, of great consequence to excite such opposition in their rear as might check them in their plan of moving southward. Inverness was occupied by a party of the insurgent forces, under Sir John Mackenzie; and Alexander Mackenzie, of Fraserdale, who assumed the authority of chief of the Frasers, in right of his lady, had marched with about four hundred of that clan to join the Earl of Marr at Perth. But the Frasers of Struy, Foyers, Culduthel, and other gentlemen of the name, refused to follow him, and maintained a sort of neutrality until the pleasure of Simon, whom they regarded as their proper chief, should be known. As this clan was powerful, both from numbers and situation,—occupying both sides of Loch Ness, and being thus masters of the communication between the north and central Highlands,—it became of the utmost consequence to detach, from the Stuarts' standard, those Frasers who had already joined Marr, and to determine the others who remained doubtful.

Fraser of Castle-Lauder was therefore despatched to invite Simon to return to Scotland, for the purpose of heading his clan in behalf of King George and the government.   The summons was joyfully obeyed, and, indeed, had been already solicited; for, on the 24th November, 1714, Simon had written to Culloden to intercede with Argyle and Isla in his favour, adding, "that it was the interest of all *between Spey and Nesse, who loved the government,* to see him at the head of the clan ready to join them:"—so that the reluctance which he has affected in his Memoirs to quitting the Jacobite interest, is only a piece of double-dyed hypocrisy.   He returned, however, to Great Britain; and here the reader may remark the strength of the clannish principle.   This chief had not been formally acknowledged as such—he had never been master of his inheritance, and his rival had enjoyed for years all the means of acquiring and securing attachment which possession could give;—there was nothing in his personal character to admire; it was stained, on the contrary, with much guilt and with dark suspicion;—and lastly, the cause which he now espoused was not that to which his followers would have inclined had they consulted their own feelings and partialities.   But he was their rightful CHIEF; and such was the strength of authority which that word implied, that those Frasers

who had stood neuter, at once declared for Simon and
his cause; and those who had marched with Fraserdale, deserted him to a man, and returned northward
to join his standard. The body of the clan thus assembled, amounted to five or six hundred. They blockaded
Inverness on one side, while the men of Culloden and
of Ross of Kilravock, who were also in arms for the
government, assailed it upon the other; so that Sir John
Mackenzie was compelled to evacuate the place under
favour of a spring tide.

Lovat lost no time in improving the advantage
which circumstances now afforded him. He had his
eye upon his rival Fraserdale's plate; but it appears
that he was anticipated by General Wrightman, who
got possession of the treasure from the person with
whom it was deposited, and who, certainly, says Mr.
Forbes's correspondent, "did not make the prize for
Lovat." Simon Fraser, however, obtained, as a reward
for his opportune services, a gift of the liferent right of
Fraserdale, in right of his wife to the Barony of Lovat,
forfeited for his share in the rebellion, and vested in the
crown. To finish the history of his law-matters, we will
here add that, having obtained this temporary right to
the estate of his ancestors, and being recognised as
Lord Lovat, he entered into a law-suit with the Mackenzies, about the right of reversion to that estate,
which lingered on till the year 1736, when it was
agreed that, in consideration of a sum of money paid
by Lord Lovat, the Mackenzies should convey to him

their reversionary interest in the barony of Lovat; and thus he had it, thanedome and all, however foully he had played for it.

Duncan Forbes, in the meanwhile, was labouring in a more honourable but far less advantageous course. Attached, by religion, by principle, by love of liberty, to the government of George I., he refused to justify the faults even of the administration which he supported. When, in 1715, the jails of England were crowded with Scottish prisoners, despoiled, and unable to procure the means of defending themselves, Forbes, to his immortal honour, set on foot a subscription to supply the unfortunate Jacobites, against whom he and his brother had borne arms so lately, with the means of making a defence. He remonstrated boldly against the arbitrary measure by which it was proposed to remove the criminals from their native country, and from the protection of their native laws, to try them in England, to them a foreign realm; and it was owing to his sturdy interference, and to that of many Scotchmen who, like him, preferred their country's rights to any party in the state, that this abuse of the constitution was prevented. The upright and patriotic conduct of Forbes was, in the first place, followed by suspicion and obliquy, but finally, by those honours and that respect which truth and fortitude seldom fail to acquire.

He was promoted to the office of Advocate-Depute, and in 1725 to that of Lord Advocate; always a situation of high power and importance, but particularly so in times of a disputed title and repeated insurrections. We find nothing in his papers to throw light upon the brief invasion of 1719, by a few Spanish troops landing in the country of the Earl of Seaforth, and joined by his clan. They were defeated at Glenshiel, with little loss on either side, and in a great measure by the Munros, Rosses, and other Whig clans, whom the influence of Duncan Forbes put into motion. Placed, as it were, on the very edge of the discontented districts, he had a difficult and even dangerous game to play. It was, says the editor of the Culloden papers, "more congenial to his nature to reclaim than to punish;" and his life was spent in keeping quiet, by means of influence, persuasion, and the interposition of friends, those warlike and independent chiefs whom presumption and political prejudice were perpetually urging to take up arms.

Lord Advocate Forbes suppressed, by his personal exertions, the desperate and alarming riots concerning the Malt tax, in 1725, and was among the patriots who saved the city of Edinburgh from the vindictive measures meditated against the metropolis, on account of the singular insurrection, called the Porteous mob. It was, indeed, one of the brightest points of this great man's character, that though the steady friend of government and good order, he was the boldest and most active mediator for his misguided fellow-subjects, when it was proposed to urge punishment beyond the bounds of correction into those of vengeance. Many other patriotic labours occupied his attention, concerning which information will be found in these papers. He was the first to give the example (since so well followed) of those effects which careful agriculture can produce, even when contending with the disadvantages of soil and climate. It was he who first proposed encouragement to the linen trade and other manufactures in Scotland.

It was he also, who first took measures for preserving and arranging the records of the kingdom of Scotland, a work which has been so actively forwarded in our own time by Lord Frederick Campbell, the Clerk Register, seconded by the deep historical and legal knowledge of the Deputy Register, Mr. Thomson. The promotion of Forbes to the high office of President of the Court of Session took place in 1737 : when called, as Lord Hardwicke expressed it, by the voice of the country, to fill the vacant chair, his appointment was hailed by all ranks as a guarantee for the impartial administration of justice, and the gradual and sound elucidation of law. It is, however, less of this great man's character, than of the Highlands of Scotland, which our review proposes to treat.

CHAPTER VIII.

THE dangers of the year 1715 occasioned several steps
towards breaking the spirit of clanship, and crushing
the power of the Highland chiefs. The first of these
was called the clan-act, which, if a vassal took arms in
any rebellion, bestowed the property of his lands upon
his superior or liege-lord, supposing him to have remained loyal, and, *vice versa*, gave the loyal vassal the
superiority or freehold right of his own lands, if he remained quiet, when his liege-lord (to use the established phrase) *went out*. Another act discharged the
personal attendances of vassals upon the summons of
the chief for sharing his sports, fighting his battles,
and garrisoning his mansion, or, in the phrase of law,
for the purposes of hunting, hosting, watching, and
warding. These badges of dependence were ordered
to be commuted for a money rent : but as the idea of
the duty remained imprinted in the minds of the clans,
it continued to be rendered regularly upon demand.

Another act was passed for disarming the Highlanders. But this measure, which would have been
otherwise effectual, was carried into execution so imperfectly, that while the Whig clans surrendered all
their arms, to show obedience to government, the

Jacobites contrived to conceal great part of theirs, to secure, when an opportunity should offer, the means of resisting it.* So that in 1745, the friends of government were found disarmed, while their enemies were in a state of preparation. The last, and by far the most effectual precaution, taken between 1715 and 1745, was the establishment of military roads through the Highlands, a work of great time and labour; but of all others the most certainly tending to civilisation. The effect of these measures was considerable upon the Highlands; and there can be little doubt, that their gradual operation would, in the course of years, or ages, perhaps, have tended to unite their inhabitants with those of the Lowlands of Scotland, as the tribes of Wales, of Ireland, and of the Borders, have gradually been blended with the rest of socity. But the system of clanship was destined to a more sudden and violent dissolution.

The steps taken by government, and the exhortations from France and Rome, kept the Highland chiefs on the alert to support the patriarchial power, which they saw was aimed at by those who governed at home, while they received encouragement from abroad to assist and defend it. Money and arms were occasionally supplied to them, and every chief and chieftain exerted himself to maintain his influence, to discourage innovation, and to banish all strangers who attempted to settle amongst them.

* See Letter from President Forbes in the Culloden Papers.

A singular instance occurred in the case of Sir
Alexander Murray of Stanhope, who, encouraged by a
very favourable prospect of lead-mines which might be
wrought to advantage, purchased a large district in the
West Highlands, called Ardnamurchan.   He laid open
rich mines at Strontian, and attempted agricultural improvements, which could not have failed at once to
improve the country, and reward the undertaker.   But
such was the hatred of the natives to a Lowland landlord, that his cattle and effects were stolen, his houses
burned, his servants wounded and killed, his own life,
and that of his family threatened, while, either from
want of evidence, or want of inclination on the part of
the constituted jurisdictions, justice was in every case
delayed or refused, until, broken in spirit and fortune,
he was compelled to relinquish this hopeful undertaking,
and to carry his unavailing complaints to the British
Parliament.   In milder times and with better auspices,
the present proprietor of that extensive tract has
carried into effect many of the proposed improvements;
yet, to his honour be it spoken, he has made the comfort
and happiness of his numerous tenantry keep pace with
the rise of his property in value.

In other places of the Highlands similar scenes were
acted ; and in general, either from the facility of
finding prey, or encouraged by the policy of the Highland chiefs, the fiercest and most lawless of the clans
and associated freebooters inhabited the mountains
nearer to the Lowlands.   Such was the information

given to Dr. Johnson by the Reverend Dr. MacQueen; which, ignorant of the circumstances, the English moralist seems to have considered as an ebullition of Highland vanity.   Nothing, however, is more certain.

The famous Rob Roy, for example, haunted the head of Loch Lomond, from which he carried on a war of plunder against the estate of the Duke of Montrose, re-treating when hard pressed into the mountains to the north-west, where the Duke of Argyle, out of ancient hatred to the Montrose family, connived at his finding refuge.   He blended in his own character the capacity of a police officer and of a freebooter—that is to say, he ensured against depredation the cattle of those Low-landers who paid him black-mail, and recovered them if stolen; and, on the other hand, he laid waste and pillaged the property of those who refused their tribute.   In virtue of his assumed character of pro-tector, he summoned the people of Lennox to pay the black-mail with as much gravity as if it had been a legal demand; and he that demurred, generally had good cause, before a week went by, to wish that he had complied.

To repress these disturbances, government adopted a remedy of a doubtful and dangerous character.   This was the raising of a number of independent companies among the Highlanders themselves, officered by the sons of chieftains, tacksmen, and such *duihné wassals* as we formerly described, and commanded by chiefs, or chieftains, to whom the pay, small as it may now seem, of a company of foot, was in those days no inconsiderable object. This *black-watch*, as it was called, traversed the country in arms day and night, became acquainted with all its recesses, and with the most desperate characters whom it contained. It must be supposed that they had the same vague opinion with other Highlanders as to the morality of the practices which they were employed to suppress; and as they often took upon them to treat with the thieves about the restoration of their booty, they were much belied if, in some instance, they did not share it with them.

At any rate, these companies were the means of fostering in the Highlanders the restless military spirit which the Clan and Disarming Acts had been intended to subdue; and as such they were used by the chiefs, who, either from attachment to the exiled family, or to their own clanish authority, did all they could to support what it was most the interest of a peaceful government to eradicate. Still, with all the dangers attending them, the independent companies were essential to the peace of the country; and when they were embodied into one regiment (the celebrated 42nd, still called the Black-Watch), and sent to Flanders without the substitution of any force of the same active description in their stead, the disaffected chiefs, rendered still more so by the loss of their companies thus withdrawn from them, had full scope for their machinations.

No man played this game more deeply than Lord

Lovat, to whom one of these independent companies had been given. He made it a main argument, to prevent the Frasers from relapsing into any habits of industry unbecoming their military character and high descent, that it was their duty to enter into his company by rotation; and as he thus procured the means, without suspicion, of training to military discipline his whole clan by turns, it soon became plain that government could not have put a more dangerous weapon into the hands of a more dangerous man.

He was, indeed, a most singular person; such as could only have arisen in a time and situation where there was a mixture of savage and civilized habits. The wild and desperate passions of his youth were now matured into a character at once bold, cautious, and crafty; loving command, yet full of flattery and dissimulation, and accomplished in all points of policy excepting that which is proverbially considered the *best.* He was at all times profuse of oaths and protestations, but chiefly, as was observed of Charles IX. of France, when he had determined in his own mind to infringe them. Like many cunning people, he often seems to have overshot his mark; while the indulgence of a temper so fierce and capricious as to infer some slight irregularity of intellect, frequently occasioned the shipwreck of his fairest schemes of self-interest. To maintain and extend his authority over a Highland clan, he showed, in miniature, alternately the arts of a Machiavel, and the tyranny of a Cæsar Borgia. He spared no means of enhancing the rents of his Lowland estate, which he bestowed liberally in maintaining the hospitality of a chief towards his Highland tenants.

Those who withstood his designs, or resisted his authority, were either worried by long and vexatious law-suits, or experienced nocturnal inroads from the banditti supposed to act under his secret direction, who houghed their cattle, burned their barn-yards, and often injured them personally. When the freebooters concerned in such outrages were arrested, the jail of Inverness was never found strong enough to hold them. And though all men well knew how this happened none dared to mention Lovat as the cause.* On the other hand, persons of the inferior order, belonging to hostile clans, who had incurred his displeasure, never found any such facilities of escape, but were indentured for the plantations, or sent to Holland as soldiers. Mr. Burt tells a very extraordinary story, which the reader may take in his own words.

" As this chief (Lovat) was walking alone, in his garden, with his dirk and pistol by his side, and a gun in his hand (as if he feared to be assassinated), and, as I was reading in his parlour, there came to me by stealth (as I soon perceived), a young fellow, who

---

* See *Letters from the North of Scotland*, vol. i., Letter III., and vol. ii., Letter XXIV. Burt gives many anecdotes of Lord Lovat, though without naming him. The gentleman whose cattle were houghed for giving sentence as an arbiter against Lord Lovat, was Cuthbert of Castlehill, and he whose house was broken into with the purpose of assassination, was Fraser of Phopachy.

accosted me with such an accent, as made me conclude he was a native of Middlesex; and every now and then he turned about, as if he feared to be observed by any of the family.

"He told me, that when his master was in London, he had made him promises of great advantage, if he would serve him as his gentleman; but though he had been there two years, he could not obtain either his wages or discharge.

"'And,' says he, 'when I ask for either of them, he tells me I know I have robbed him, and nothing is more easy for him than to find, among these Highlanders, abundant evidence against me (innocent as I am); and then my fate must be a perpetual jail, or transportation: and there is no means for me to make my escape, being here in the midst of his clan and never suffered to go far from home.'

"You will believe I was much affected with the melancholy circumstance of the poor young man; but told him, that my speaking for him would discover his complaint to me, which might enrage his master; and, in that case, I did not know what might be the consequence to him.

"Then, with a sorrowful look, he left me, and (as it happened) in very good time."—Letter x.

In his family, Lord Lovat exercised similar tyranny. The eldest son, a hopeful and excellent young man, was the constant object of his jealousy; and his last wife, though nearly related to the family of Argyle, was treated by him with so much cruelty, that the interference of her relations became necessary. We have heard that a lady, the intimate friend of her youth, was instructed to visit Lady Lovat, as if by accident, to ascertain the truth of those rumours concerning her husband's conduct, which had reached her family. She was received by Lord Lovat with an extravagant affectation of welcome, and with many assurances of the happiness which his lady would receive from seeing her. The chief then went to the lonely tower in which Lady Lovat was secluded without decent clothes, and even without sufficient nourishment. He laid a dress before her becoming her rank, commanded her to put it on, to appear, and to receive her friend as if she were the mistress of the house, in which she was, in fact, a naked and half-starved prisoner. And such was the strict watch he maintained, and the terror his character inspired, that the visitor durst not ask, nor Lady Lovat communicate, any thing respecting her real situation. It was, however, ascertained by other means, and a separation took place.

We have seen the versatility of Lord Lovat in earlier life; the services which he rendered George I. during the year 1715; the advantages of his independent company; his rank as Lord-lieutenant of Inverness-shire, besides the gratuity of a pension, were boons granted to secure his allegiance to the house of Brunswick; but it was quickly found that with ambitious turbulence, which was even too great for his sense of self-interest, he was still engaged in obscure and secret negotiations with the exiled family. In 1737, he received a visit from Colonel Roy Stuart, an emissary of the Chevalier, and gave great cause of suspicion, both by that circumstance and by the quantity of swords, targets, and other arms, which he was observed to import from abroad. Yet it seems inconsistent with his character to have joined irretrievably in a cause so desperate, had he not fallen into a sort of open disgrace with the government.

About 1739, his independent company and pension were both withdrawn, contrary to the advice of President Forbes, who foresaw the effects of the pecuniary loss and public disgrace upon a spirit so interested, so haughty, and so dangerous. The crisis of civil contention accordingly approached; and the tempting offer of a dukedom and the lieutenancy of all the counties north of the Spey, overcame Lovat's worldly wisdom, although few men had more. He paused, indeed, upon finding that Charles had landed with such a slender force; and his letters to President Forbes, prior to the battle of Prestonpans, indicate an intention of supporting the established government. The victory obtained by the Chevalier determined his sentiments; and in presence of many of his vassals, being urged by an emissary of the Prince to " throw off the mask," he flung down his hat and drank success to the young adventurer by the title which he claimed, and confusion to the White Horse and all his adherents. But with the Machiavelism inherent in his nature, he resolved that his own personal interest in the insurrection should be as little evident as possible, and determined that his son, whose safety he was bound, by the laws of God and man, to prefer to his own, should be his stalking-horse, and, in case of need, his scape-goat.

Meanwhile, his friend and neighbour, President Forbes, was labouring to dissuade the Highland chiefs from joining in this rash expedition. With many of the most powerful he found means to prevail, particularly with the laird of Macleod, and Sir Alexander MacDonald of Sleat, whose numerous tribes would have made a formidable addition to the Chevalier's army. With Lovat he used his utmost influence; and the letters between them are among the most entertaining in this volume. Lovat is, at first, vehement in his demand for arms to protect his vassals and put his country into a state of defence. By-and-by he is compelled to admit that many of his followers were eager to enter into the rebellion; and lastly, that his eldest son had been seduced to put himself at their head, and had actually mustered four hundred Frasers, and marched off with them to join the Chevalier. It appears, from the evidence of Fraser of Dunballoch and others, upon Lord Lovat's trial, that all this while the threats and arguments of the father were urging the son (afterwards the highly esteemed General Fraser) to a step of which he disapproved, and that he was still more disgusted by the duplicity and versatility with which his father qualified it.

Meanwhile, between this wily and unprincipled chief, and others of a more violent and open character, the President was placed in a condition of difficulty and danger, which shall be described in his own words.

" The prospect (of dissuading the chiefs) was at first very flattering, and the errand I came on had no appearance of difficulty; but the rebell's successes at Edr. and Preston-pans soon changed the scene. All Jacobites, how prudent soever, became mad; all doubtfull people became Jacobites: and all bankrupts became heroes, and talk'd nothing but hereditary rights and victory; and, what was more grievious to men of gallantry, and if you will believe me much mor mischievous to the publick, all the fine ladys, if you will except one or two, became passionately fond of the young adventurer, and used all their arts and industry for him in the most intemperate manner. Under these circumstances, I found myself almost alone, without troops, without arms, without money or credite; provided without no means to prevent extream folly, except pen and ink, a tongue, and some reputation; and if you will except MacLeod, whom I sent for from the isle of Sky, supported by nobody of common sense or courage."—P. 250.

Yet, in these circumstances, by indefatigable exertion, and by liberally contributing both money and credit to the cause, he was enabled to assemble such a force at Inverness, as served to distract the councils, and interrupt the supplies of the Chevalier, and to pave the way for the downfall of his cause. Lovat, in the meanwhile, after exhausting every subterfuge, fled from Inverness, where he had surrendered himself on a kind of parole, and did not return to his house until, by the northward march of the Chevalier's army, and other events, the friends of government were for a time forced to abandon Inverness.

CHAPTER IX.

Prince Charles at Dounie Castle—Lord Lovat's last days—Endeared Memory of President Forbes—Severities on the Highlanders after the 1745 Rising—The good and bad points in Clanship—Highland Romance.

IT was not till after the battle of Culloden, that Lovat beheld the unfortunate prince in whose cause he had sacrificed himself. A lady, who then a girl, was residing in Lord Lovat's family, described to us the unexpected appearance of Prince Charles and his flying attendants, at Castle Dounie. The wild and desolate vale, on which she was gazing with indolent composure, was at once so suddenly filled with horsemen riding furiously towards the castle, that, impressed with the belief that they were fairies, who, according to Highland tradition, are visible to men only from one twinkle of the eye-lid to another, she strove to refrain from the vibration, which she believed would occasion the strange and magnificent apparition to become invisible.

To Lord Lovat it brought a certainty more dread-
ful than the presence of fairies, or even demons. The
tower on which he had depended had fallen to crush
him, and he only met the Chevalier to exchange mutual
condolences. Yet Lovat lost neither heart nor judgment. Obliged to fly, though now so old and infirm
that he was transported on the shoulders of his
followers, he still advised the chiefs to keep together
their men, and either to prosecute a mountain war, or
show so bold a countenance as might obtain honourable terms of peace. But this design miscarried ; and
after skulking from isle to isle, he was at length
discovered within the trunk of a hollow tree, and
carried on board the *Furnace* ship of war.

Lord Lovat maintained, to the last, his character of
versatility and hardihood. In a letter to the Duke of
Cumberland, he endeavoured to excite his compassion,
by telling him how often he had carried him in his
arms when a child, offered to make such discoveries as
would be of an hundred times more advantage to
government than the sacrifice of an old grey-head, but
concluded—he was

> —————"in utrumque paratus,
> Seu versare dolos, seu certæ incumbere morti."

During his previous confinement, during the course
of his trial, and even till the last hour of his life, his bold
and firm demeanour, the satirical causticity of his
vein of humour, and the respect commanded by energy

of character, even when they abused, secured him a
degree of interest, of a very different nature, but not
much inferior to that which Balmerino gained by his
undaunted steadiness, and Kilmarnock by his affecting
penitence.   At his execution, two expressions marked
that he was Lovat still—when the scaffold fell and
killed several persons.

"Ay, ay" (exclaimed he, just about to die), "the
mair mischief the better sport."

And he chose for his last words the "Dulce et decorum" of Horace.   Such sentiments in the mouth of
such a character, and at such a moment, seem prepos-
terous almost to incredibility; but Lovat is not the
only criminal whose conduct was guided by self-
interest during life, and who has yet assumed at his
death, the manners and language of a patriot.

The reader will naturally expect to hear of the re-
wards and honours which were showered on President
Forbes for his admirable conduct during a period so
difficult and dangerous.   Of these we learn nothing.
But we suspect that the memory of his services was
cancelled by the zeal with which, after the victory, he
pressed the cause of clemency.   We have heard that
when this venerable judge, as well became his station,
mentioned the laws of the country, he was answered,
not, as the editor supposes, by the Duke of Albemarle,
but by a personage greater still :

"What laws ?—I'll make a brigade give laws ! "

That his repeated intercessions in favour of those

who, from prejudice of education, or a false sense of
honour, had joined the Chevalier, were taken in bad
part; and his desire to preserve to the Highlanders a
dress fitted to their occupations, was almost construed
into disaffection;—in fine, that he died broken in spirit
by witnessing the calamities of his country, and im-
poverished in estate, by the want of that very money
which he had, in the hour of need, frankly advanced
to levy troops for the service of government. But he
left behind him a name endeared, even in these days
of strife and bitterness, to enemies as to friends, and
doubly to be honoured by posterity, for that impartiality which uniformly distinguished between the
cause of the country and political party. By a sort of
posthumous ingratitude, the privilege of distilling,
without payment of duty, upon his barony of Ferrintosh, an immunity conferred to compensate his father's
losses and reward his services at the revolution, and
hence termed by Burns, "Loyal Forbes's chartered
boast," was wrenched from the family by government,
in 1785, for a most inadequate recompense.

[An eminent antiquary, to whom the publisher applied for a copy of the view of Old Culloden House as
it stood in 1746, and for the purpose of illustrating this
volume, has kindly supplied the following particulars:
"The original proprietors of Culloden, were *Strachans*,
a family from Aberdeenshire: the last of whom was
succeeded by his three daughters, as heiresses por-
tioners, who divided his estates among them; so that

the barony split into three thirds, and thus it is described to this day.   The era of this event must have
been *circiter* A.D. 1520.   Fifty years subsequently
thereto, Mackintosh of Dunachtoun (now of Mackintosh), purchased the entire barony from these ladies
and their husbands.   In 1630, or thereabouts, Mackintosh sold the barony to Duncan Forbes, merchant in
Inverness, a younger son of a respectable family in
Aberdeenshire; I incline to think, of Brux, or Craigie-
var.   Duncan became member of Parliament for the
burgh of Inverness, and acquired much property in its
neighbourhood.   He continued to reside in the old
chateau of the Strachans, and he also built a handsome
residence in the Castle Wynd of the town, over the
lintel of which his own and his wife's initials may yet
be seen.   It adjoined the 'great *slated* house,' originally sold by Henry Duvar, prior of the monastery of
Inverness, in 1517, to Laurence Robertson of Inches,
and subsequently the property of the Lovat family;
perhaps the first *slated* house in the capital of the
Highlands, for even till 1571 the churches were *thatched.*
To Duncan Forbes succeeded John of Culloden, who
likewise represented the burgh for many years in Parliament, and, like his father, was its provost.   Duncan
his son again succeeded him, and obtained the privilege of distilling whisky in his barony of Ferrintosh
from William and Mary.   'Bumper John,' as his *soubri-
quet* went, from his excessive hospitality, was his heir;
to him followed the justly esteemed patriot, Duncan

Forbes, his younger brother, afterwards Lord President of the Court of Session. Burt, in his Letters from the North, commemorates the joyous hilarity of the 'castle' of Culloden when tenanted by the elder brother. 'It is the custom of that house, at the first visit or introduction, to take up your freedom by cracking his nut (as he terms it)—that is, a cocoa shell, which holds a pint, filled with champaigne, or such other sort of wine as you shall choose. You may guess from the *introduction*, at the contents of the *volume*. Few go away sober at any time; and for the greatest part of his guests, in the conclusion, they cannot go at all.' Though less hilariously disposed than his merry kinsman, the good President also could relax from the sterner cares of life, and in the classic shades of his beloved 'Bunchrew'—(a small property on the opposite line of the Murray Frith, which he acquired before his accession to the paternal domain)—many a happy hour fled with those he esteemed."]

If we touch upon the severities exercised with a most unsparing hand, after the insurrection of 1745, during the course of which the Highlanders had conducted themselves with humanity and moderation, it is but to repel an expression of the editor of the Culloden papers, who, after admitting the existence of these "acts of atrocity," strangely subjoins, that "*no blame can attach to the Duke of Cumberland for them.*"

We, on the contrary, maintain that to the general of the victorious army, and to no other, is imputable every consequence of the orders which he issues; and if a veil is drawn over the conduct of the Duke of Cumberland, it is out of no respect or tenderness to the memory of that prince, but in justice to the far different sentiments of many members of his illustrious family, who knew how to prize faith and honour even in the enemies of their house, and who have often testified respect for the memory of those who risked their all because their mistaken loyalty demanded the sacrifice, and who, in prosecuting their enterprise, did nothing in hate, but all in honour.

When the Princess of Wales, mother of his present Majesty, mentioned, with some appearance of censure, the conduct of Lady Margaret Macdonald of Sleat, who harboured and concealed the Prince when, in the extremity of peril, he threw himself on her protection.

"And would not you, madam," answered Prince Frederick, "have done the same in the like circumstances?—I hope—I am sure you would."

Besides the great measure of restoring the forfeited estates of the chiefs, our venerable sovereign* showed, on many occasions, how little his heart was capable of nourishing dislike against those who had acted upon principle against the authority of his family. The support which he afforded to the exiled branch of the Stuarts will form a bright trait in his history; and secluded as he now is from his government and people,

* [King George III.]

we may, as of a deceased monarch, relate one of those trifling *traits* which marked the generous kindness of his disposition. His Majesty was told of a gentleman of family and fortune, in——— shire, that, far from taking the oath of allegiance to him, he had never been known to name or permit him to be named as king in his presence.

"Carry my compliments to him," said the King, "and say that I respect his steadiness of principle; or, as he may not receive my compliments as King of England, present them as those of the Elector of Hanover."

And he never afterwards saw the gentleman from whom the anecdote is derived, without inquiring after the health of the venerable recusant, and reiterating his wish to be remembered to him. The same kindness to the memory of those who hazarded themselves for the Stuart cause has been inherited by the present administrator of royal authority, and to him, as to his father, their descendants have been and are prompt to repay it.

We now draw to a conclusion. We have shown the power of clanship in its most unamiable form, as devolving on a man whom neither faith nor gratitude could bind,—a tyrant to his family, a terror to his vassals;—selfish enough to shelter his own safety by imputing to his son the crime to which he compelled him, and a traitor to the political interests which he embraced and abandoned alternately. Such a char-

acter ranks with the Ras Michael and Fasil of Bruce,
and rather belongs to the Galla, or the Agows, than to
the Scottish Highlands.   It might have been our lot to
present patriarchal authority in a very different light,
as exercised by Allan Cameron of Lochiel, who, to the
high spirit, courage, and loyalty of a Highland chief,
added the manners of an accomplished gentleman and
the morals of a good Christian.   Beloved by his neighbours, he was the terror of the oppressor and the
refuge of the oppressed; he suppressed in his clan
every license which could disturb the public, while his
bounty and encouragement rendered peaceful industry
more profitable to them than the hostile and predatory
habits of their ancestors.   And when he took his last
and fatal step it was with no view of self-interest—no
desire of individual fame or honour—but in the pure
spirit of one who devoted himself to a cause which he
well knew to be desperate, because he deemed himself
called upon, by his honour and allegiance, to obey the
summons of the prince who threw himself upon so rash
a hazard.

Clanship, therefore, like other modes of government,
differed in complexion, according to the character by
whom the authority was exercised; but it may be
observed in general, that though despotic in principle,
its duties were reciprocal; and that the chief who
neglected to protect and maintain his people, was in
danger of being disowned and deserted by them.
Clanship, however, with its good, and evil, is now no

more. Its harsher features disappeared, after the pro-
mulgation of the laws in 1748, which struck at the
root of the chiefs' authority, both patriarchal and
feudal.

The execution of young Robert Roy, Sergeant More
Cameron, and other leaders of predatory bands of
Highlanders, with the banishment of the yet more distinguished Barrisdale, checked their habits of violence.
A milder race arose;—the Highlanders with whom our
youth was conversant, cultivating sedulously the
means of subsistence which their country afforded, and
converting the broadsword into the ploughshare, and
the spear into the herdsman's crook, yet preserving an
aptitude to military habits, and an enthusiastic energy
of character derived from the recollections of former
days, and fostered by the tales of the grey-headed
veterans, who looked back with regret to the days
when each man's arms clattered round him when he
walked the hills. Among these men, the spirit of clanship subsisted no longer indeed as a law of violence,
but still as a law of love. They maintained, in many
instances, their chiefs at their own expense; and they
embodied themselves in regiments, that the head of the
family might obtain military preferment. Whether
and how these marks of affection have been rewarded,
is a matter of deep and painful enquiry. But while it
subsisted, this voluntary attachment to the chief was,
like the ruins of his feudal castle, more interesting than

when clanship subsisted in its entire vigour, and re-
minded us of the expression of the poet :—

——————————" Time
Has mouldered into beauty many a tower
Which, when it frown'd with all its battlements,
Was only terrible."——————

Some such distinction between Highlanders and
Lowlanders in this respect, would long have subsisted,
had it been fostered by those who, we think, were most
interested in maintaining it. The dawn of civilisation
would have risen slowly on the system of Highland
Society ; and as the darker and harsher shades were
already dispelled, the romantic contrast and variety
reflected upon ancient and patriarchal usages, by the
general diffusion of knowledge, would, like the brilliant
colours of the morning clouds, have survived for some-
time, ere blended with the general mass of ordinary
manners. In many instances, Highland proprietors
have laboured with laudable and humane precaution to
render the change introduced by a new mode of
cultivation gentle and gradual, and to provide, as far
as possible, employment and protection for those
families who were thereby dispossessed of their ancient
habitations. But in other, and in but too many instances, the glens of the Highlands have been drained,
not of their superfluity of population, but of the whole
mass of the inhabitants, dispossessed by an unrelenting
avarice, which will be one day found to have been as
shortsighted as it is unjust and selfish.

Meanwhile the Highlands may become the fairy ground for romance and poetry, or subject of experiment for the professors of speculation, political and economical.—But if the hour of need should come—and it may not, perhaps, be far distant—the pibroch may sound through the deserted region, but the summons will remain unanswered.   The children who have left her will re-echo from a distant shore the sounds with which they took leave of their own—*Ha til, ha til, ha til, mi tulidh !*—" We return—we return—we return—no more *!* "

Life and Exploits of Rob Roy
and
Historical Account of the
Clan Macgregor

LIFE AND EXPLOITS

OF

ROB ROY

AND

HISTORICAL ACCOUNT

OF THE

CLAN MACGREGOR.

CHAPTER I.

Rob Roy compared to Robin Hood—Peculiar History of the Clan MacGregor—Their descent and wrongs—Especial Statutes against the Clan—Feud between the MacGregors and the Colquhouns— The Battle of Glenfruin.

THE singular character whose name is given above, maintained, through good report and bad report, a wonderful degree of importance in popular recollection. This cannot be ascribed to the distinction of his birth, which, though that of a gentleman, had in it nothing of high destination, and gave him little right to command in his clan. Neither, though he lived a busy, restless, and enterprising life, were his feats equal to those of other freebooters who have been less distinguished. He owed his fame in a great measure to his residing on the very verge of the Highlands, and playing such pranks in the beginning of the 18th century, as are usually ascribed to Robin Hood in the middle ages,— and that within forty miles of Glasgow, a great commercial city, the seat of a learned university. Thus a character like his, blending the wild virtues, the subtle policy, and unrestrained license of an American Indian, was flourishing in Scotland during the Augustan age of Queen Anne and George I. Addison, it is probable, or Pope, would have been considerably surprised if they had known that there existed in the same island with them a personage of Rob Roy's peculiar habits and profession. It is this strong contrast betwixt the civilized and cultivated mode of life on the one side of the Highland line, and the wild and lawless adventures which were habitually undertaken and achieved by one who dwelt on the opposite side of that ideal boundary, which creates the interest attached to his name. Hence it is that even yet,

> " Far and near, through vale and hill,
> Are faces that attest the same,
> And kindle like a fire new stirr'd,
> At sound of Rob Roy's name."

There were several advantages which Rob Roy enjoyed, for sustaining to advantage the character which he assumed.

The most prominent of these was his descent from,

and connexion with, the Clan MacGregor, so famous
for their misfortunes, and the indomitable spirit with
which they maintained themselves as a clan, linked and
banded together in spite of the most severe laws,
executed with unheard-of rigour against those who
bore this forbidden surname. Their history was that
of several others of the original Highland clans, who
were suppressed by more powerful neighbours, and
either extirpated, or forced to secure themselves by
renouncing their own family appellation, and assuming
that of the conquerors. The peculiarity in the story
of the MacGregors, is their retaining, with such tena-
city, their separate existence and union as a clan under
circumstances of the utmost urgency. The history of
the tribe is briefly as follows: But we must premise
that the tale depends in some degree on tradition,
therefore, excepting when written documents are
quoted, it must be considered as in some degree
dubious.

The sept of MacGregor claimed a descent from
Gregor, or Gregorius, third son, it is said, of Alpin
King of Scots, who flourished about 787. Hence their
original patronymic is MacAlpine, and they are usually
termed the Clan Alpine. An individual tribe of them
retains the same name. They are accounted one of
the most ancient clans in the Highlands, and it is
certain they were a people of original Celtic descent,
and occupied at one period very extensive possessions
in Perthshire and Argyleshire, which they imprudently

continued to hold by the *coir a glaive*, that is, the right
of the sword. Their neighbours, the Earls of Argyle
and Broadalbane, in the meanwhile, managed to have
the lands occupied by the MacGregors engrossed in
those charters which they easily obtained from the
Crown ; and thus constituted a legal right in their
own favour, without much regard to its justice. As
opportunity occurred of annoying or extirpating their
neighbours, they gradually extended their own domains,
by usurping, under the pretext of such royal grants,
those of their more uncivilized neighbours. A Sir
Duncan Campbell of Lochow, known in the Highlands
by the name of *Donacha Dhu nan Churraichd*, that is,
Black Duncan with the Cowl, it being his pleasure to
wear such a head-gear, is said to have been peculiarly
successful in those acts of spoliation upon the clan
MacGregor.

The devoted sept, ever finding themselves iniquit-
ously driven from their possessions, defended themselves
by force, and occasionally gained advantages, which
they used cruelly enough. This conduct, though
natural, considering the country and time, was studi-
ously represented at the capital as arising from an
untamable and innate ferocity, which nothing, it was
said, could remedy, save cutting off the tribe of Mac-
Gregor root and branch.

In an act of Privy Council at Stirling, 22nd September, 1563, in the reign of Queen Mary, commission is
granted to the most powerful nobles, and chiefs of the

clans, to pursue the clan Gregor with fire and sword. A similar warrant in 1562, not only grants the like powers to Sir John Campbell of Glenorchy, the descendant of Duncan with the Cowl, but discharges the lieges to receive or assist any of the clan Gregor, or afford them, under any colour whatever, meat, drink, or clothes.

An atrocity which the clan Gregor committed in 1589, by the murder of John Drummond of Drummond-ernoch, a forester of the royal forest of Glenartney, is elsewhere given, with all its horrid circumstances. The clan swore upon the severed head of the murdered man, that they would make common cause in avowing the deed. This led to an act of the Privy Council, directing another crusade against the " wicked clan Gregor, so long continuing in blood, slaughter, theft, and robbery," in which letters of fire and sword are denounced against them for the space of three years. The reader will find this particular fact illustrated in the Introduction to the novel of the Legend of Montrose.

Other occasions frequently occurred, in which the MacGregors testified contempt for the laws, from which they had often experienced severity, but never protection. Though they were gradually deprived of their possessions, and of all ordinary means of procuring subsistence, they could not, nevertheless, be supposed likely to starve for famine, while they had the means of taking from strangers what they considered as rightfully their own. Hence they became

versed in predatory forays, and accustomed to bloodshed. Their passions were eager, and, with a little
management on the part of some of their most powerful neighbours, they could easily be *hounded out*, to use
an expressive Scottish phrase, to commit violence, of
which the wily instigators took the advantage, and
left the ignorant MacGregors an undivided portion of
blame and punishment. This policy of pushing on the
fierce clans of the Highlands and Borders to break the
peace of the country, is accounted by the historian one
of the most dangerous practices of his own period, in
which the MacGregors were considered as ready agents.

Notwithstanding these severe denunciations, which
were acted upon in the same spirit in which they were
conceived, some of the clan still possessed property,
and the chief of the name in 1592 is designed Allaster
MacGregor of Glenstrae. He is said to have been a
brave and active man ; but, from the tenor of his con-
fession at his death, appears to have been engaged in
many and desperate feuds, one of which finally proved
fatal to himself and many of his followers. This was
the celebrated conflict at Glenfruin, near the south-
western extremity of Loch Lomond, in the vicinity of
which the MacGregors continued to exercise much
authority by the *coir a glaive*, or right of the strongest,
which we have already mentioned.

There had been a long and bloody feud betwixt the
MacGregors and the Laird of Luss, head of the family
of Colquhoun, a powerful race on the lower part of

Loch Lomond. The MacGregors' tradition affirms that the quarrel began on a very trifling subject. Two of the MacGregors being benighted, asked shelter in a house belonging to a dependent of the Colquhouns, and were refused. They then retreated to an out-house, took a wedder from the fold, killed it, and supped off the carcase, for which (it is said) they offered payment to the proprietor. The Laird of Luss seized on the offenders, and, by the summary process which feudal barons had at their command, had them both condemned and executed. The MacGregors verify this account of the feud by appealing to a proverb current amongst them, execrating the hour (*Mult dhu an Carbail ghil*) that the black wedder with the white tail was ever lambed. To avenge this quarrel, the Laird of MacGregor assembled his clan, to the number of three or four hundred men, and marched towards Luss from the banks of Loch Long, by a pass called *Raid na Gael*, or the Highlandman's Pass.

Sir Humphrey Colquhoun received early notice of this incursion, and collected a strong force, more than twice the number of that of the invaders. He had with him the gentlemen of the name of Buchanan, with the Grahams, and other gentry of the Lennox, and a party of the citizens of Dunbarton, under command of Tobias Smollett, a magistrate, or bailie, of that town, and ancestor of the celebrated author.

The parties met in the valley of Glenfruin, which signifies the Glen of Sorrow, a name that seemed to anticipate the event of the day, which, fatal to the conquered party, was at least equally so to the victors, the "babe unborn" of clan Alpine having reason to repent it.   The MacGregors, somewhat discouraged by the appearance of a force much superior to their own, were cheered on to the attack by a Seer, or second-sighted person, who professed that he saw the shrouds of the dead wrapt around their principal opponents. The clan charged with great fury on the front of the enemy, while John MacGregor, with a strong party, made an unexpected attack on the flank.   A great part of the Colquhouns' force consisted in cavalry, which could not act in the boggy ground.   They were said to have disputed the field manfully, but were at length completely routed, and a merciless slaughter was exercised on the fugitives, of whom betwixt two and three hundred fell on the field, and in the pursuit.   If the MacGregors lost, as is averred, only two men slain in the action, they had slight provocation for an indiscriminate massacre.

It is said that their fury extended itself to a party of students for clerical orders, who had imprudently come to see the battle.   Some doubt is thrown on this fact, from the indictment against the chief of the clan Gregor being silent on the subject, as is the historian Johnston, and a Professor Ross, who wrote an account of the battle twenty-nine years after it was fought.   It is, however, constantly averred by the tradition of the country, and a stone where the deed was done is called

Leck-a-Mhinisteir, the Minister or Clerk's Flag-stone. The MacGregors impute this cruel action to the ferocity of a single man of their tribe, renowned for size and strength, called Dugald, *Ciar Mhor*, or the great Mouse-coloured Man. He was MacGregor's foster-brother, and the chief committed the youths to his charge, with directions to keep them safely till the affray was over. Whether fearful of their escape, or incensed by some sarcasms which they threw on his tribe, or whether out of mere thirst for blood, this savage, while the other MacGregors were engaged in the pursuit, poniarded his helpless and defenceless prisoners. When the chieftain, on his return, demanded where the youths were, the *Ciar* (pronounced Kiar) *Mhor* drew out his bloody dirk, saying in Gaelic,

"Ask that, and God save me!"

The latter words allude to the exclamation which his victims used when he was murdering them. It would seem, therefore, that this horrible part of the story is founded on fact, though the number of youths so slain is probably exaggerated in the Lowland accounts. The common people say that the blood of the Ciar Mhor's victims can never be washed off the stone. When MacGregor learnt their fate he expressed the utmost horror at the deed, and upbraided his foster-brother with having done that which would occasion the destruction of him and his clan. This homicide was the ancestor of Rob Roy, and the tribe from which he was descended. He lies buried at the church of

Fortingal, where his sepulchre, covered with a large stone, is still shown, and where his great strength and courage are the theme of many traditions.

I have been informed, that, at no very remote period, it was proposed to take this large stone, which marks the grave of Dugald Ciar Mohr, and convert it to the purpose of the lintel of a window, the threshold of a door, or some such mean use. A man of the clan Mac-Gregor, who was somewhat deranged, took fire at this insult; and when the workmen came to remove the stone, planted himself upon it, with a broad axe in his hand, swearing he would dash out the brains of any one who should disturb the monument. Athletic in person, and insane enough to be totally regardless of consequences, it was thought best to give way to his humour; and the poor madman kept sentinel on the stone day and night, till the proposal of removing it was entirely dropped.

The above is the account which I find in a manuscript history of the clan MacGregor, of which I was indulged with a perusal by Donald MacGregor, Esq., late Major of the 33rd regiment, where great pains have been taken to collect traditions and written documents concerning the family. But an ancient and constant tradition, preserved among the inhabitants of the country, and particularly those of the clan Mac-Farlane, relieves Dugal Ciar Mohr of the guilt of murdering the youths, and lays the blame on a certain Donald or Duncan Lean, who performed the act of cruelty, with the assistance of a gillie who attended him, named Charlioch, or Charlie. They say that the homicides dared not again join their clan, but that they resided in a wild and solitary state as outlaws, in an unfrequented part of the MacFarlanes' territory. Here they lived for some time undisturbed, till they committed an act of brutal violence on two defenceless women, a mother and a daughter of the MacFarlane clan. In revenge for this atrocity, the MacFarlanes hunted them down and shot them. It is said the young ruffian, Charlioch, might have escaped, being remarkably swift of foot. But his crime became his punishment, for the female whom he had outraged had defended herself desperately, and had stabbed him with his own dirk on the thigh. He was lame from the wound, and was the more easily overtaken and killed. I incline to think that this last is the true edition of the story, and that the guilt was transferred to Dugald Ciar Mohr, as a man of higher name. Or it is possible these subordinate persons had only executed his orders.

MacGregor's brother was one of the very few of the tribe who was slain. He was buried near the field of battle, and the place is marked by a rude stone, called the Grey Stone of MacGregor.

Sir Humphrey Colquhoun, being well mounted, escaped for the time to the castle of Banochar, or Benechra. It proved no sure defence, however, for he was shortly after murdered in a vault of the castle, the family annals say by the MacGregors, though other accounts charge the deed upon the MacFarlanes.

CHAPTER II.

Results of the Battle of Glenfruin—The Chief surrenders to the Duke
of Argyle—The Duke betrays him—Trial and Execution at Edinburgh—The MacGregors under King James I. and Charles I.—
Later Times—Genealogy of Rob Roy.

THIS battle of Glenfruin, and the severity which the
victors exercised in the pursuit, was reported to King
Jame VI. in a manner the most unfavourable to the
clan Gregor, whose general character, being that of
lawless though brave men, could not much avail them
in such a case. That James might fully understand
the extent of the slaughter, the widows of the slain to
the number of eleven score, in deep mourning, riding
upon white palfreys, and each bearing her husband's bloody shirt on a spear, appeared at Stirling,
in presence of a monarch peculiarly accessible to such
sights of fear and sorrow, to demand vengeance for the
death of their husbands, upon those by whom they had
been made desolate.

The remedy resorted to was at least as severe as the
cruelties which it was designed to punish. By an act
of the Privy Council, dated 3rd April, 1603, the name
of MacGregor was expressly abolished, and those who
had hitherto borne it were commanded to change it for
other surnames, the pain of death being denounced
against those who should call themselves Gregor or
MacGregor, the names of their fathers. Under the
same penalty, all who had been at the conflict of Glen-

fruin, or accessory to marauding parties charged in the act, were prohibited from carrying weapons, except a pointless knife to eat their victuals. By a subsequent act of Council, 24th June, 1613, death was denounced against any persons of the tribe formerly called Mac-Gregor, who should presume to assemble in greater numbers than four. Again, by an act of Parliament, 1617, chap. 26, these laws were continued, and extended to the rising generation, in respect that great numbers of the children of those against whom the acts of Privy Council had been directed, were stated to be then approaching to maturity, who, if permitted to resume the name of their parents, would render the clan as strong as it was before.

The execution of those severe acts was chiefly intrusted in the west to the Earl of Argyle, and the powerful clan of Campbell, and to the Earl of Athole and his followers, in the more eastern Highlands of Perthshire. The MacGregors failed not to resist with the most determined courage; and many a valley in the West and North Highlands retains memory of the severe conflicts, in which the prescribed clan sometimes obtained transient advantages, and always sold their lives dearly. At length the pride of Allaster MacGregor, the chief of the clan, was so much lowered by the sufferings of his people, that he resolved to surrender himself to the Earl of Argyle, with his principal followers, on condition that they should be sent out of Scotland. If the unfortunate chief's own account be true, he had more reasons than one for expecting some favour from the Earl, who had in secret advised and encouraged him to many of the desperate actions for which he was now called to so severe a reckoning. But Argyle, as an old Birrell expresses himself, kept a Highlandman's promise with them, fulfilling it to the ear, and breaking it to the sense. MacGregor was sent under a strong guard to the frontier of England, and being thus, in the literal sense, sent out of Scotland, Argyle was judged to have kept faith with him, though the same party which took him there brought him back to Edinburgh in custody.

MacGregor of Glenstrae was tried before the Court of Justiciary, 20th January, 1604, and found guilty He appears to have been instantly conveyed from the bar to the gallows; for Birrell, of the same date, reports that he was hanged at the Cross, and, for distinction's sake, was suspended higher by his own height than two of his kindred and friends. On the 18th of February following, more men of the MacGregors were executed, after a long imprisonment, and several others in the beginning of March.

The Earl of Argyle's service, in conducing to the surrender of the insolent and wicked race and name of MacGregor, notorious common malefactors, and in the in-bringing of MacGregor, with a great many of the leading men of the clan, worthily executed to death for their offences, is thankfully acknowledged by act of Parliament, 1607, chap. 16, and rewarded with a grant of twenty chalders of victual out of the lands of Kintire.

The MacGregors, notwithstanding the letters of fire and sword, and orders for military execution repeatedly directed against them by the Scottish legislature, who apparently lost all the calmness of conscious dignity and security, and could not even name the outlawed clan without vituperation, showed no inclination to be blotted out of the roll of clanship. They submitted to the law, indeed, so far as to take the names of the neighbouring families amongst whom they happened to live, nominally becoming, as the case might render it most convenient, Drummonds, Campbells, Grahams, Buchanans, Stewarts, and the like; but to all intents and purposes of combination and mutual attachment, they remained the clan Gregor, united together for right or wrong, and menacing with the general vengeance of their race, whomsoever committed aggressions against any individual of their number.

They continued to take and give offence with as little hesitation as before the legislative dispersion which had been attempted, as appears from the preamble to statute 1633, chapter 30, setting forth, that the clan Gregor, which had been suppressed and reduced to quietness by the great care of the late King James of eternal memory, had nevertheless broken out again, in the counties of Perth, Stirling, Clackmannan, Monteith, Lennox, Angus, and Mearns; for which reason the statute re-establishes the disabilities attached to the clan, and grants a new commission for enforcing the laws against that wicked and rebellious race.

Notwithstanding the extreme severities of King James I. and Charles I. against this unfortunate people, who were rendered furious by proscription, and then punished for yielding to the passions which had been wilfully irritated, the MacGregors to a man attached themselves during the civil war to the cause of the latter monarch. Their bards have ascribed this to the native respect of the MacGregors for the crown of Scotland, which their ancestors once wore, and have appealed to their armorial bearings, which display a pine-tree, crossed satire wise with a naked sword, the point of which supports a royal crown. But, without denying that such motives may have had their weight, we are disposed to think, that a war which opened the low country to the raids of the clan Gregor would have more charms for them than any inducement to espouse the cause of the Covenanters, which would have brought them into contact with Highlanders as fierce as themselves, and having as little to lose. Patrick MacGregor, their leader, was the son of a distinguished chief, named Duncan Abbarach, to whom Montrose wrote letters as to his trusty and special friend, expressing his reliance on his devoted loyalty, with an assurance, that when once his Majesty's affairs were placed upon a permanent footing, the grievances of the clan MacGregor should be redressed.

At a subsequent period of these melancholy times,

we find the clan Gregor claiming the immunities of
other tribes, when summoned by the Scottish Parliament to resist the invasion of the Commonwealth's
army, in 1651. On the last day of March in that year,
a supplication to the King and Parliament, from Calum
MacCondachie Vich Euen, and Euen MacCondachie
Euen, in their own name, and that of the whole name
of MacGregor, set forth, that while, in obedience to the
orders of Parliament, enjoining all clans to come out in
the present service under their chieftains, for the
defence of religion, king, and kingdoms, the petitioners
were drawing their men to guard the passes at the head
of the river Forth, they were interfered with by the
Earl of Athole and the Laird of Buchanan, who had
required the attendance of many of the clan Gregor
upon their arrays. This interference was, doubtless,
owing to the change of name, which seems to have
given rise to the claim of the Earl of Athole and the
Laird of Buchanan to muster the MacGregors under
their banners, as Murrays or Buchanans. It does not
appear that the petition of the MacGregors, to be permitted to come out in a body as other clans, received
any answer. But upon the Restoration, King Charles,
in the first Scottish Parliament of his reign, (statute
164, chap. 195,) annulled the various acts against the
clan Gregor, and restored them to the full use of their
family name, and the other privileges of liege subjects,
setting forth, as a reason for this lenity, that those who
were formerly designed MacGregors, had, during the

late troubles, conducted themselves with such loyalty and affection to his Majesty, as might justly wipe off all memory of former miscarriages, and take away all marks of reproach for the same.

It is singular enough, that it seems to have aggravated the feelings of the non-conforming Presbyterians, when the penalties which were most unjustly imposed upon themselves were relaxed towards the poor MacGregors; so little are the best men, any more than the worst, able to judge with impartiality of the same measures, as applied to themselves, or to others. Upon the Restoration, an influence inimical to this unfortunate clan, said to be the same with that which afterwards dictated the massacre of Glencoe, occasioned the re-enaction of the penal statutes against the Mac-Gregors. There are no reasons given why these highly penal acts should have been renewed; nor is it alleged that the clan had been guilty of late irregularities. Indeed, there is some reason to think that the clause was formed of set purpose, in a shape which should elude observation; for, though containing conclusions fatal to the rights of so many Scottish subjects, it is neither mentioned in the title nor the rubric of the Act of Parliament in which it occurs, and is thrown briefly in at the close of the statute 1693, chap. 61, entitled an Act for the Justiciary in the Highlands.

It does not, however, appear that after the Revolution the acts against the clans were severely enforced; and in the latter half of the eighteenth century, they

were not enforced at all. Commissioners of supply
were named in Parliament by the prescribed title of
MacGregor, and decrees of courts of justice were
pronounced, and legal deeds entered into, under the
same appellative. The MacGregors, however, while
the laws continued in the statute book, still suffered
under the deprivation of the name which was their
birth-right, and some attempts were made for the
purpose of adopting another, MacAlpine or Grant being
proposed as the title of the whole clan in future. No
agreement, however, could be entered into; and the
evil was submitted to as a matter of necessity, until
full redress was obtained from the British Parliament,
by an act abolishing for ever the penal statutes which
had been so long imposed upon this ancient race.
This statute, well merited by the services of many a
gentleman of the clan in behalf of their King and
country was passed, and the clan proceeded to act upon
it with the same spirit of ancient times, which had
made them suffer severely under a deprivation that
would have been deemed of little consequence by a
great part of their fellow subjects.

They entered into a deed recognising John Murray
of Lanrick, Esq., (afterwards Sir John MacGregor,
Baronet), representative of the family of Glencarnock,
as lawfully descended from the ancient stock and
blood of the Lairds and Lords of MacGregor, and
therefore acknowledged him as their chief on all lawful occasions and causes whatsoever. This deed was

subscribed by eight hundred and twenty-six persons
of the name of MacGregor, capable of bearing arms. A
great many of the clan during the last war formed
themselves into what was called the Clan Alpine
regiment, raised in 1799, under the command of their
Chief, and his brother Colonel MacGregor.

Having briefly noticed the history of this clan, which
presents a rare and interesting example of the indelible
character of the patriarchal system, the author must
now offer some notices of the individual who gives
name to these volumes.

In giving an account of a Highlander, his pedigree is
first to be considered. That of Rob Roy was deduced
from Ciar Mohr, the great mouse-coloured man, who is
accused by tradition of having slain the young students
at the battle of Glenfruin.

Without puzzling ourselves and our readers with the
intricacies of Highland genealogy, it is enough to say,
that after the death of Allaster MacGregor of Glenstrae,
the clan, discouraged by the unremitting persecution
of their enemies, seem not to have had the means of
placing themselves under the command of a single
CHIEF. According to their places of residence and
immediate descent, the several families were led and
directed by *Chieftains*, which, in the Highland accepta-
tion, signifies the head of a particular branch of a tribe,
in opposition to *Chief*, who is the leader and commander
of the whole name.

The family and descendants of Dugald Ciar Mohr

lived chiefly in the mountains between Loch Lomond and Loch Katrine, and occupied a good deal of property there, whether by sufferance, by the right of the sword, which it was never safe to dispute with them, or by legal titles of various kinds, it would be useless to enquire and unnecessary to detail. Enough, there they certainly were; a people whom their most powerful neighbours were desirous to conciliate, their friendship in peace being very necessary to the quiet of the vicinage, and their assistance in war equally prompt and effectual.

CHAPTER III.

Rob Roy's Birth and Early Years—His property of Craig Royston—
Ruined by his partner—His wife—Predatory war against the
Duke of Montrose—His general appearance and character.

ROB ROY MACGREGOR CAMPBELL, which last name he bore in consequence of the Acts of Parliament abolishing his own, was the younger son of Donald MacGregor of Glengyle, said to have been a Lieutenant-Colonel, (probably in the service of James II.) by his wife, a daughter of Campbell of Glenfalloch. Rob's own designation was of Inversnaid; but he appears to have acquired a right of some kind or other to the property or possession of Craig Royston, a domain of rock and forest, lying on the east side of Loch Lomond, where that beautiful lake stretches into the dusky mountains of Glenfalloch.

The time of his birth is uncertain. But he is said to have been active in the scences of war and plunder which succeeded the Revolution; and tradition affirms him to have been the leader in a predatory incursion into the parish of Kippen, in the Lennox, which took place in the year 1691. It was of almost a bloodless character, only one person losing his life; but from the extent of the depredation, it was long distinguished by the name of the Her'-ship, or devastation, of Kippen.* The time of his death is also uncertain, but as he is said to have survived the year 1733, and died an aged man, it is probable he may have been twenty-five about the time of the Her'-ship of Kippen, which would assign his birth to the middle of the 17th century.

In the more quiet times which succeeded the Revolution, Rob Roy, or Red Robert, seems to have exerted his active talents, which were of no mean order, as a drover or trader in cattle to a great extent. It may well be supposed that in those days no Lowland, much less English drovers, ventured to enter the Highlands. The cattle, which were the staple commodity of the mountains, were escorted down to fairs, on the borders of the Lowlands, by a party of Highlanders, with their arms rattling around them; and who dealt, however, in all honour and good faith with their Southern

* See Statistical Account of Scotland, vol. xviii. page 332. Parish of Kippen.

customers. A fray, indeed, would sometimes arise, when the Lowlandmen, chiefly Borderers, who had to supply the English market, used to dip their bonnets in the next brook, and wrapping them round their hands, oppose their cudgels to the naked broadswords, which had not always the superiority. I have heard from aged persons, who had been engaged in such affrays, that the Highlanders used remarkably fair play, never using the point of the sword, far less their pistols or daggers; so that

> With many a stiff thwack and many a bang,
> Hard crabtree and cold iron rang.

A slash or two, or a broken head, was easily accommodated, and as the trade was of benefit to both parties, trifling skirmishes were not allowed to interrupt its harmony. Indeed it was of vital interest to the Highlanders, whose income, so far as derived from their estates, depended entirely on the sale of black cattle; and a sagacious and experienced dealer benefited not only himself, but his friends and neighbours, by his speculations. Those of Rob Roy were for several years so successful, as to inspire general confidence, and raise him in the estimation of the country in which he resided.

His importance was increased by the death of his father, in consequence of which he succeeded to the management of his nephew Gregor MacGregor of Glengyle's property, and, as his tutor, to such influence with the clan and following as was due to the representative of Dougal Ciar. Snch influence was the more uncontrolled, that this family of the MacGregors seem to have refused adherence to MacGregor of Glencarnock, the ancestor of the present Sir Ewan MacGregor, and asserted a kind of independence.

It was at this time that Rob Roy acquired an interest by purchase, wadset, or otherwise, to the property of Craig Royston already mentioned. He was in particular favour, during this prosperous period of his life, with his nearest and most powerful neighbour, James first Duke of Montrose, from whom he received many marks of regard. His Grace consented to give his nephew and himself a right of property on the estates of Glengyle and Inversnaid, which they had till then only held as kindly tenants. The Duke, also, with a view to the interest of the country and his own estate, supported our adventurer by loans of money to a considerable amount, to enable him to carry on his speculations in the cattle trade.

Unfortunately, that species of commerce was and is liable to sudden fluctuations; and Rob Roy was—by a sudden depression of markets, and, as a friendly tradition adds, by the bad faith of a partner named MacDonald, whom he had imprudently received into his confidence, and intrusted with a considerable sum of money—rendered totally insolvent. He absconded, of course,—not empty-handed, if it be true, as stated in an advertisement for his apprehension, that he had in his possession sums to the amount of L.1000 sterling, obtained from several noblemen and gentlemen under pretence of purchasing cows for them in the Highlands. This advertisement appeared in June 1712, and was several times repeated. It fixes the period when Rob Roy exchanged his commercial adventures for speculations of a very different complexion.*

He appears at this period first to have removed, from his ordinary dwelling at Inversnaid, ten or twelve Scots miles (which is double the number of English) farther into the Highlands, and commenced the lawless sort of life which he afterwards followed. The Duke of Montrose, who conceived himself deceived and cheated by MacGregor's conduct, employed legal means to recover the money lent to him. Rob Roy's landed property was attached by the regular form of legal procedure, and his stock and furniture made the subject of arrest and sale.

It is said that this diligence of the law, as it is called in Scotland, which the English more bluntly term distress, was used in this case with uncommon severity, and that the legal satellites, not usually the gentlest persons in the world, had insulted MacGregor's wife, in a manner which would have aroused a milder man than he to thoughts of unbounded vengeance. She was a woman of fierce and haughty temper, and is not unlikely to have disturbed the officers in the execution

* See Appendix, No. I.

of their duty, and thus to have incurred ill treatment, though, for the sake of humanity, it is to be hoped that the story sometimes told is a popular exaggeration. It is certain that she felt extreme anguish at being expelled from the banks of Loch Lomond, and gave vent to her feelings in a fine piece of pipe-music, still well known to amateurs by the name of "Rob Roy's Lament."

The fugitive is thought to have found his first place of refuge in Glen Dochart, under the Earl of Breadalbane's protection; for though that family had been active agents in the destruction of the MacGregors in former times, they had of late years sheltered a great many of the name in their old possessions. The Duke of Argyle was also one of Rob Roy's protectors, so far as to afford him, according to the Highland phrase, wood and water—the shelter, namely, that is afforded by the forests and lakes of an inaccessible country.

The great men of the Highlands in that time, besides being anxiously ambitious to keep up what was called their Following, or military retainers, were also desirous to have at their disposal men of resolute character, to whom the world and the world's law were no friends, and who might at times ravage the lands or destroy the tenants of a feudal enemy, without bringing responsibility on their patrons. The strife between the names of Campbell and Graham, during the civil wars of the seventeenth century, had been stamped with mutual loss and inveterate enmity. The death of the

great Marquis of Montrose on the one side, the defeat
at Inverlochy, and cruel plundering of Lorn, on the
other, were reciprocal injuries not likely to be forgotten. Rob Roy was, therefore, sure of refuge in the
country of the Campbells, both as having assumed
their name, as connected by his mother with the family
of Glenfalloch, and as an enemy to the rival house of
Montrose. The extent of Argyle's possessions, and the
power of retreating thither in any emergency, gave
great encouragement to the bold schemes of revenge
which he had adopted.

This was nothing short of the maintenance of a predatory war against the Duke of Montrose, whom he
considered as the author of his exclusion from civil
society, and of the outlawry to which he had been
sentenced by letters of horning and caption, (legal
writs so called,) as well as the seizure of his goods,
and adjudication of his landed property. Against his
Grace, therefore, his tenants, friends, allies, and
relatives, he disposed himself to employ every means
of annoyance in his power; and though this was a
circle sufficiently extensive for active depredation,
Rob, who professed himself a Jacobite, took the
liberty of extending his sphere of operations against
all whom he chose to consider as friendly to the re-
volutionary government, or to that most obnoxious of
measures—the Union of the Kingdoms. Under one or
other of these pretexts, all his neighbours of the Lowlands who had any thing to lose, or were unwilling to

compound for security, by paying him an annual sum for protection or forbearance, were exposed to his ravages.

The country in which this private warfare, or system of depredation, was to be carried on, was until opened up by roads, in the highest degree favourable for his purpose. It was broken up into narrow valleys, the habitable part of which bore no proportion to the huge wildernesses of forest, rocks, and precipices by which they were encircled, and which was, moreover, full of inextricable passes, morasses, and natural strengths, unknown to any but the inhabitants themselves, where a few men acquainted with the ground were capable, with ordinary address, of baffling the pursuit of numbers.

The opinions and habits of the nearest neighbours to the Highland line were also highly favourable to Rob Roy's purpose. A large proportion of them were of his own clan of MacGregor, who claimed the property of Balquhidder, and other Highland districts, as having been part of the ancient possessions of their tribe; though the harsh laws, under the severity of which they had suffered so deeply, had assigned the ownership to other families. The civil wars of the seventeenth century had accustomed these men to the use of arms, and they were peculiarly brave and fierce from remembrance of their sufferings. The vicinity of a comparatively rich Lowland district gave also great temptations to incursion. Many belonging to other clans, habituated to contempt of industry, and to the use of arms, drew towards an unprotected frontier which promised facility of plunder; and the state of the country, now so peaceable and quiet, verified at that time the opinion which Dr. Johnson heard with doubt and suspicion, that the most disorderly and law-less districts of the Highlands were those which lay nearest to the Lowland line.　There was, therefore, no difficulty in Rob Roy, descended of a tribe which was widely dispersed in the country we have described, collecting any number of followers whom he might be able to keep in action, and to maintain by his proposed operations.

He himself appears to have been singularly adapted for the profession which he proposed to exercise.　His stature was not of the tallest, but his person was un-commonly strong and compact.　The greatest peculiari-ties of his frame were the breadth of his shoulders, and the great and almost disproportioned length of his arms ; so remarkable, indeed, that it was said he could, without stooping, tie the garters of his Highland hose, which are placed two inches below the knee.　His countenance was open, manly, stern at periods of danger, but frank and cheerful in his hours of festivity. His hair was dark red, thick, and frizzled, and curled short around the face.　His fashion of dress showed, of course, the knees and upper part of the leg, which was described to me as resembling that of a Highland bull, hirsute, with red hair, and evincing muscular strength similar to that animal.　To these personal qualifications must be added a masterly use of the Highland sword, in which his length of arm gave him great advantage, and a perfect and intimate knowledge of all the recesses of the wild country in which he laboured, and the character of the various individuals, whether friendly or hostile, with whom he might come in contact.

His mental qualities seem to have been no less adapted to the circumstances in which he was placed. Though the descendant of the blood-thirsty Ciar Mohr, he inherited none of his ancestor's ferocity. On the contrary, Rob Roy avoided every appearance of cruelty, and it is not averred that he was ever the means of unnecessary bloodshed, or the actor in any deed which could lead the way to it. His schemes of plunder were contrived and executed with equal boldness and sagacity, and were almost universally successful, from the skill with which they were laid, and the secrecy and rapidity with which they were executed. Like Robin Hood of England, he was a kind and gentle robber, and, while he took from the rich, was liberal in relieving the poor. This might in part be policy; but the universal tradition of the country speaks it to have arisen from a better motive. All whom I have conversed with, and I have in my youth seen some who knew Rob Roy personally, gave him the character of a benevolent and humane man " in his way."

CHAPTER IV.

Wordsworth on Rob Roy—Rob Roy at Doune—Combat at Shiling Hill—Rob Roy's lieutenant—A narrow escape— Rob Roy's depredations—The MacGregors in the 1715 Rising—The affair of the Boats.

His ideas of morality were those of an Arab chief, being such as naturally arose out of his wild education. Supposing Rob Roy to have argued on the tendency of the life which he pursued, whether from choice or from necessity, he would doubtless have assumed to himself the character of a brave man, who, deprived of his natural rights by the partiality of laws, endeavoured to assert them by the strong hand of natural power; and he is most felicitously described as reasoning thus, in the high-toned poetry of my gifted friend Wordsworth :

> Say, then, that he was wise as brave,
>   As wise in thought as bold in deed ;
> For in the principles of things
>   *He* sought his moral creed.
>
> Said generous Rob, " What need of Books ?
>   Burn all the statutes and their shelves !
> They stir us up against our kind,
>   And worse, against ourselves.
>
> " We have a passion, make a law,
>   Too false to guide us or control ;
> And for the law itself we fight
>   In bitterness of soul.
>
> " And puzzled, blinded, then we lose
>   Distinctions that are plain and few ;
> These find I graven on my heart,
>   That tells me what to do.

" The creatures see of flood and field,
    And those that travel on the wind ;
With them no strife can last ; they live
    In peace, and peace of mind.

" For why ? Because the good old rule
    Sufficeth them ; the simple plan,
That they should take who have the power,
    And they should keep who can.

" A lesson which is quickly learn'd,
    A signal through which all can see ;
Thus, nothing here provokes the strong
    To wanton cruelty.

" And freakishness of mind is check'd,
    He tamed who foolishly aspires,
While to the measure of his might
    Each fashions his desires.

" All kinds and creatures stand and fall
    By strength of prowess or of wit ;
'Tis God's appointment who must sway,
    And who is to submit.

" Since then," said Robin, " right is plain,
    And longest life is but a day,
To have my ends, maintain my rights,
    I'll take the shortest way."

And thus among these rocks he lived,
    Through summer's heat and winter's snow :
The eagle, he was lord above,
    And Rob was lord below.

We are not, however, to suppose the character of
this distinguished outlaw to be that of an actual hero,
acting uniformly and consistently on such moral principles as the illustrious bard who, standing by his grave,
has vindicated his fame. On the contrary, as is

common with barbarous chiefs, Rob Roy appears to have mixed his professions of principle with a large alloy of craft and dissimulation, of which his conduct during the civil war is sufficient proof. It is also said, and truly, that although his courtesy was one of his strongest characteristics, yet sometimes he assumed an arrogance of manner which was not easily endured by the high-spirited men to whom it was addressed, and drew the daring outlaw into frequent disputes, from which he did not always come off with credit. From this it has been inferred, that Rob Roy was more of a bully than a hero, or at least that he had, according to the common phrase, his fighting days. Some aged men who knew him well, have described him also as better at a *taich-tulzie*, or scuffle within doors, than in mortal combat. The tenor of his life may be quoted to repel this charge; while, at the same time, it must be allowed, that the situation in which he was placed rendered him prudently averse to maintaining quarrels, where nothing was to be had save blows, and where success would have raised up against him new and powerful enemies, in a country where revenge was still considered as a duty rather than a crime. The power of commanding his passions, on such occasions, far from being inconsistent with the part which Mac-Gregor had to perform, was essentially necessary, at the period when he lived, to prevent his career from being cut short.

I may here mention one or two occasions on which

Rob Roy appears to have given way in the manner alluded to. My late venerable friend, John Ramsay of Ochtertyre, alike eminent as a classical scholar and as an authentic register of the ancient history and manners of Scotland, informed me, that on occasion of a public meeting at a bonfire in the town of Doune, Rob Roy gave some offence to James Edmondstone of Newton, the same gentleman who was unfortunately concerned in the slaughter of Lord Rollo, (See Maclaurin's Criminal Trials, No IX.,) when Edmondstone compelled MacGregor to quit the town on pain of being thrown by him into the bonfire.

"I broke one of your ribs on a former occasion," said he, "and now, Rob, if you provoke me farther, I will break your neck."

But it must be remembered that Edmondstone was a man of consequence in the Jacobite party, as he carried the royal standard of James VII. at the battle of Sherrif-muir, and also, that he was near the door of his own mansion-house, and probably surrounded by his friends and adherents. Rob Roy, however, suffered in reputation for retiring under such a threat.

Another well-vouched case is that of Cunningham of Boquhan.

Henry Cunningham, Esq. of Boquhan, was a gentleman of Stirlingshire, who, like many *exquisites* of our own time, united a natural high spirit and daring character with an affectation of delicacy of address and manners amounting to foppery.* He chanced to be in company with Rob Roy, who, either in contempt of Boquhan's supposed effeminacy, or because he thought him a safe person to fix a quarrel on, (a point which Rob's enemies alleged he was wont to consider,) insulted him so grossly that a challenge passed between them. The goodwife of the clachan had hidden Cunningham's sword, and, while he rummaged the house in quest of his own or some other, Rob Roy went to the Shieling Hill, the appointed place of combat, and paraded there with great majesty, waiting for his antagonist. In the meantime, Cunningham had rummaged out an old sword, and, entering the ground of contest in all haste, rushed on the outlaw with such unexpected fury that he fairly drove him off the field, nor did he show himself in the village again for some time. Mr. MacGregor Stirling has a softened account of this anecdote in his new edition of Nimmo's Stirlingshire; still he records Rob Roy's discomfiture.

* His courage and affectation of foppery were united, which is less frequently the case, with a spirit of innate modesty. He is thus described in Lord Binning's satirical verses, entitled " Argyle's Levee."

> " Six times had Harry bow'd unseen
>   Before he dared advance ;
> The Duke then, turning round well pleased,
>   Said, 'Sene you've been in France,
> A more polite and jaunty man
>   I never saw before ;'
> Then Harry bow'd, and blush'd, and bow'd,
>   And strutted to the door."

See a Collection of Original Poems, by Scotch Gentlemen, Vol. II., p. 125.

Occasionally Rob Roy suffered disasters, and incurred great personal danger. On one remarkable occasion he was saved by the coolness of his lieutenant, Macanaleister, or Fletcher, the *Little John* of his band—a fine active fellow, of course, and celebrated as a marksman. It happened that MacGregor and his party had been surprised and dispersed by a superior force of horse and foot, and the word was given to "split and squander." Each shifted for himself, but a bold dragoon attached himself to pursuit of Rob, and overtaking him, struck at him with his broadsword. A plate of iron in his bonnet saved the MacGregor from being cut down to the teeth; but the blow was heavy enough to bear him to the ground, crying as he fell,

" O, Macanaleister, is there naething in her? " (*i.e.* in the gun). The trooper, at the same time exclaiming,

" D—n ye, your mother never wrought your nightcap!" had his arm raised for a second blow, when Macanaleister fired, and the ball pierced the dragoon's heart.

Such as he was, Rob Roy's progress in his occupation is thus described by a gentleman of sense and talent, who resided within the circle of his predatory wars, had probably felt their effects, and speaks of them, as might be expected, with little of the forbearance with which, from their peculiar and romantic character, they are now regarded.

" This man (Rob Roy MacGregor) was a person of sagacity, and neither wanted stratagem nor address;

and, having abandoned himself to all licentiousness, set himself at the head of all the loose, vagrant, and desperate people of that clan, in the west end of Perth and Stirlingshires, and infested those whole countries with thefts, robberies, and depredations. Very few who lived within his reach (that is, within the distance of a nocturnal expedition) could promise to themselves security, either for their persons or effects, without subjecting themselves to pay him a heavy and shameful tax of *black mail*. He at last proceeded to such a degree of audaciousness, that he committed robberies, raised contributions, and resented quarrels, at the head of a very considerable body of armed men, in open day and in the face of the government." *

The extent and success of these depredations cannot be surprising, when we consider that the scene of them was laid in a country where the general law was neither enforced nor respected.

Having recorded that the general habit of cattle-stealing had blinded even those of the better classes to the infamy of the practice, and that as men's property consisted entirely in herds, it was rendered in the highest degree precarious, Mr. Grahame adds,—

" On these accounts there is no culture of ground, no improvement of pastures, and, from the same reasons, no manufactures, no trade ; in short, no industry. The

* Mr. Grahame of Gartmore's Causes of the Disturbances in the Highlands. See Jamieson's edition of Burt's Letters from the North of Scotland, Appendix, Vol. II., p. 348.

people are extremely prolific, and therefore so numerous, that there is not business in that country, according to its present order and economy, for the one-half of them. Every place is full of idle people, accustomed to arms, and lazy in every thing but rapines and depredations. As *buddel* or *aquavitæ* houses are to be found every where through the country, so in these they saunter away their time, and frequently consume there the returns of their illegal purchases. Here the laws have never been executed, nor the authority of the magistrate ever established. Here the officer of the law neither dare nor can execute his duty, and several places are about thirty miles from lawful persons. In short, here is no order, no authority, no government."

The period of the Rebellion, 1715, approached soon after Rob Roy had attained celebrity. His Jacobite partialities were now placed in opposition to his sense of the obligations which he owed to the indirect protection of the Duke of Argyle. But the desire of " drowning his sounding steps amid the din of general war," induced him to join the forces of the Earl of Mar, although his patron, the Duke of Argyle, was at the head of the army opposed to the Highland insurgents.

The MacGregors, a large sept of them at least, that of Ciar Mohr, on this occasion, were not commanded by Rob Roy, but by his nephew already mentioned, Gregor MacGregor, otherwise called James Grahame of Glengyle, and still better remembered by the Gaelic epithet of *Ghlune Dhu, i.e.* Black Knee, from a black spot on one of his knees, which his Highland garb rendered visible. There can be no question, however, that being then very young, Glengyle must have acted on most occasions by the advice and direction of so experienced a leader as his uncle.

The MacGregors assembled in numbers at that period, and began even to threaten the Lowlands towards the lower extremity of Loch Lomond. They suddenly seized all the boats which were upon the lake, and, probably with a view to some enterprise of their own, drew them overland to Inversnaid, in order to intercept the progress of a large body of west-country whigs who were in arms for the government, and moving in that direction.

The whigs made an excursion for the recovery of the boats. Their forces consisted of volunteers from Paisley, Kilpatrick, and elsewhere, who, with the assistance of a body of seamen, were towed up the river Leven in long-boats belonging to the ships of war then lying in the Clyde. At Luss they were joined by the forces of Sir Humphry Colquhoun, and James Grant, his son-in-law, with their followers, attired in the Highland dress of the period, which is picturesquely described. "At night they arrived at Luss, where they were joined by Sir Humphry Colquhoun of Luss, and James Grant of Plascander, his son-in-law, followed by forty or fifty stately fellows in their short hose and belted plaids, armed each of them with a well-fixed gun on his shoulder, a strong handsome target, with a

sharp-pointed steel of above half an ell in length
screwed into the navel of it, on his left arm, a sturdy
claymore by his side, and a pistol or two, with a dirk
and knife, in his belt."*   The whole party crossed to
Craig-Royston, but the MacGregors did not offer combat. If we are to believe the account of the expedition
given by the historian Rae, they leaped on shore at
Craig-Royston with the utmost intrepidity, no enemy
appearing to oppose them, and, by the noise of their
drums, which they beat incessantly, and the discharge
of their artillery and small arms, terrified the Mac-
Gregors, whom they appear never to have seen, out of
their fastnesses, and caused them to fly in a panic to the
general camp of the Highlanders at Strath Fillan.
The Loch Lomond expedition was judged worthy to
form a separate pamphlet, which I have not seen, but,
as quoted by the historian Rae, it must be delectable.

   " On the morrow, being Thursday the 13th, they
went on their expedition, and about noon came to
Inversnaid, the place of danger, where the Paisley men
and those of Dumbarton, and several of the other companies, to the number of an hundred men, with the
greatest intrepidity leapt on shore, got up to the top of
the mountains, and stood a considerable time, beating
their drums all the while; but no enemy appearing,
they went in quest of their boats, which the rebels had
seized, and having casually lighted on some ropes and
oars hid among the shrubs, at length they found the

* *Rae's History of the Rebellion,* 4to. p. 287.

boats drawn up a good way on the land, which they hurled down to the loch.   Some of them as were not damaged they carried off with them, and such as were, they sank and hewed to pieces.   That same night they returned to Luss, and thence next day to Dumbarton, from whence they had first set out, bringing along with them the whole boats they found in their way on either side of the loch, and in the creeks of the isles, and mooring them under the cannon of the castle.   During this expedition the pinnaces discharging their patararoes, and the men their small-arms, made such a thundering noise, through the multiplied rebounding echoes of the vast mountains on both sides of the loch, that the MacGregors were cowed and frighted away to the rest of the rebels who were encamped at Strath Fillan."*   The low-country men succeeded in getting possession of the boats, at a great expenditure of noise and courage, and little risk of danger.

After this temporary removal from his old haunts, Rob Roy was sent by the Earl of Mar to Aberdeen, to raise, it is believed, a part of the clan Gregor, which is settled in that country.   These men were of his own family (the race of the Ciar Mohr).   They were the descendants of about three hundred MacGregors whom the Earl of Murray, about the year 1624, transported from his estates in Monteith to oppose against his enemies the MacIntoshes, a race as hardy and restless as they were themselves.

* *Rae's History of the Rebellion*, 4to. p. 287.

CHAPTER V.

Rob Roy and the Professor—The MacGregors at the Battle of Sheriff-
muir—Rob turns the Battle to personal advantage—Resumes his
warfare with Montrose—The Duke's Factor—Rob lifts the rents.

BUT while in the city of Aberdeen, Rob Roy met a
relation of a very different class and character from
those whom he was sent to summon to arms. This was
Dr. James Gregory, (by descent a MacGregor,) the
patriarch of a dynasty of professors distinguished for
literary and scientific talent, and the grandfather of the
late eminent physician and accomplished scholar, Professor Gregory of Edinburgh. This gentleman was at
the time Professor of Medicine in King's College,
Aberdeen, and son of Dr. James Gregory, distinguished
in science as the inventor of the reflecting telescope.
With such a family it may seem our friend Rob could
have had little communion. But civil war is a species
of misery which introduces men to strange bedfellows.
Dr. Gregory thought it a point of prudence to claim
kindred, at so critical a period, with a man so formidable and influential. He invited Rob Roy to his house,
and treated him with so much kindness, that he produced in his generous bosom a degree of gratitude
which seemed likely to occasion very inconvenient
effects.

The Professor had a son about eight or nine years
old,—a lively, stout boy of his age,—with whose
appearance our Highland Robin Hood was much taken.

On the day before his departure from the house of his learned relative, Rob Roy, who had pondered deeply how he might requite his cousin's kindness, took Dr. Gregory aside, and addressed him to this purport :—

"My dear kinsman, I have been thinking what I could do to show my sense of your hospitality. Now, here you have a fine spirited boy of a son, whom you are ruining by cramming him with your useless book-learning, and I am determined, by way of manifesting my great good-will to you and yours, to take him with me, and make a man of him."

The learned Professor was utterly overwhelmed when his warlike kinsman announced his kind purpose, in language which implied no doubt of its being a proposal which would be, and ought to be, accepted with the utmost gratitude. The task of apology or explanation was of a most delicate description; and there might have been considerable danger in suffering Rob Roy to perceive that the promotion with which he threatened the son was, in the father's eyes, the ready road to the gallows. Indeed, every excuse which he could at first think of—such as regret for putting his friend to trouble with a youth who had been educated in the Lowlands, and so on—only strengthened the chieftain's inclination to patronise his young kinsman, as he supposed they arose entirely from the modesty of the father. He would for a long time take no apology, and even spoke of carrying off the youth by a certain degree of kindly violence, whether his father consented or not. At length the perplexed Professor pleaded that his son was very young, and in an infirm state of health, and not yet able to endure the hardships of a mountain life; but that in another year or two he hoped his health would be firmly established, and he would be in a fitting condition to attend on his brave kinsman, and follow out the splendid destinies to which he opened the way. This agreement being made, the cousins parted,—Rob Roy pledging his honour to carry his young relation to the hills with him on his next return to Aberdeenshire, and Dr. Gregory, doubtless, praying in his secret soul that he might never see Rob's Highland face again.

James Gregory, who thus escaped being his kinsman's recruit, and in all probability his henchman, was afterwards Professor of Medicine in the College, and, like most of his family, distinguished by his scientific acquirements. He was rather of an irritable and pertinacious disposition; and his friends were wont to remark, when he showed any symptom of these foibles, "Ah! this comes of not having been educated by Rob Roy."

The connexion between Rob Roy and his classical kinsman did not end with the period of Rob's transient power. At a period considerably subsequent to the year 1715, he was walking in the Castle Street of Aberdeen, arm in arm with his host, Dr. James Gregory, when the drums in the barracks suddenly beat to arms, and soldiers were seen issuing from the barracks.

"If these lads are turning out," said Rob, taking leave of his cousin with great composure, "it is time for me to look after my safety."

So saying, he dived down a close, and, as John Bunyan says, "went upon his way and was seen no more."

The first of these anecdotes, which brings the highest pitch of civilisation so closely in contact with the half-savage state of society, I have heard told by the late distinguished Dr. Gregory, and the members of his family have had the kindness to collate the story with their collections and family documents, and furnish the authentic particulars. The second rests on the recollection of an old man, who was present when Rob took French leave of his literary cousin on hearing the drums beat, and communicated the circumstance to Mr. Alexander Forbes, a connexion of Dr. Gregory by marriage.

We have already stated that Rob Roy's conduct during the insurrection of 1715 was very equivocal. His person and followers were in the Highland army, but his heart seems to have been with the Duke of Argyle's. Yet the insurgents were constrained to trust to him as their only guide, when they marched from Perth towards Dumblane, with the view of crossing the Forth at what are called the Fords of Frew, and when they themselves said he could not be relied upon.

This movement to the westward, on the part of the

insurgents, brought on the battle of Sheriff-muir,
indecisive indeed in its immediate results, but of which
the Duke of Argyle reaped the whole advantage.   In
this action, it will be recollected that the right wing of
the Highlanders broke and cut to pieces Argyle's left
wing, while the clans on the left of Mar's army, though
consisting of Stewarts, Mackenzies, and Camerons, were
completely routed.   During this medley of flight and
pursuit, Rob Roy retained his station on a hill in the
centre of the Highland position ; and though it is said
his attack might have decided the day, he could not be
prevailed upon to charge.   This was the more unfortunate for the insurgents, as the leading of a party of
the Macphersons had been committed to MacGregor.
This, it is said, was owing to the age and infirmity of
the chief of that name, who, unable to lead his clan in
person, objected to his heir-apparent, Macpherson of
Nord, discharging his duty on that occasion ; so that
the tribe, or a part of them, were brigaded with their
allies the MacGregors.   While the favourable moment
for action was gliding away unemployed, Mar's positive
orders reached Rob Roy that he should presently
attack.   To which he coolly replied,

"No, no ! if they cannot do it without me, they cannot do it with me."

"One of the Macphersons, named Alexander, one of
Rob's original profession, *videlicet* a drover, but a man
of great strength and spirit, was so incensed at the

inactivity of his temporary leader, that he threw off his plaid, drew his sword, and called out to the clansmen,

" Let us endure this no longer ! if he will not lead you, I will."

" Rob Roy replied, with great coolness,

" Were the question about driving Highland stots or kyloes, Sandie, I would yield to your superior skill ; but as it respects the leading of men, I must be allowed to be the better judge."—

" Did the matter respect driving Glen-Eigas stots," answered the Macpherson, " the question with Rob would not be, which was to be last, but which was to be foremost."

" Incensed at this sarcasm, MacGregor drew his sword, and they would have fought upon the spot if their friends on both sides had not interfered. But the moment of attack was completely lost. Rob did not, however, neglect his own private interest on the occasion. In the confusion of an undecided field of battle, he enriched his followers by plundering the baggage and the dead on both sides.

The fine old satirical ballad on the battle of Sheriff-muir does not forget to stigmatize our hero's conduct on this memorable occasion.

> Rob Roy he stood watch
> On a hill for to catch
>   The booty, for aught that I saw, man ;
> For he ne'er advanced
> From the place where he stanced,
>   Till nae mair was to do there at a', man.

Notwithstanding the sort of neutrality which Rob
Roy had continued to observe during the progress of
the Rebellion, he did not escape some of its penalties.
He was included in the act of attainder, and the house
in Breadalbane, which was his place of retreat, was
burned by General Lord Cadogan, when, after the
conclusion of the insurrection, he marched through the
Highlands to disarm and punish the offending clans.
But upon going to Inveraray with about forty or fifty
of his followers, Rob obtained favour, by an apparent
surrender of their arms to Col. Patrick Campbell of
Finnah, who furnished them and their leader with pro-
tections under his hand.   Being thus in a great measure
secured from the resentment of government, Rob Roy
established his residence at Craig-Royston, near Loch
Lomond, in the midst of his own kinsmen, and lost no
time in resuming his private quarrel with the Duke of
Montrose.   For this purpose, he soon got on foot as
many men, and well armed too, as he had yet commanded.   He never stirred without a body-guard of
ten or twelve picked followers, and without much effort
could increase them to fifty or sixty.

The Duke was not wanting in efforts to destroy this
troublesome adversary.   His Grace applied to General
Carpenter, commanding the forces in Scotland, and by
his orders three parties of soldiers were directed from
the three different points of Glasgow, Stirling, and Finlarig near Killin.   Mr. Graham of Killearn, the Duke of
Montrose's relation and factor, Sheriff-depute also of

Dumbartonshire, accompanied the troops, that they might act under the civil authority, and have the assistance of a trusty guide well acquainted with the hills. It was the object of these several columns to arrive about the same time in the neighbourhood of Rob Roy's residence, and surprise him and his followers. But heavy rains, the difficulties of the country, and the good intelligence which the Outlaw was always supplied with, disappointed their well-concerted combination. The troops, finding the birds were flown, avenged themselves by destroying the nest. They burned Rob Roy's house, though not with impunity, for the Mac-Gregors, concealed among the thickets and cliffs, fired on them, and killed a grenadier.

Rob Roy avenged himself for the loss which he sustained on this occasion by an act of singular audacity. About the middle of November, 1716, John Graham of Killearn, already mentioned as factor of the Montrose family, went to a place called Chapel Errock, where the tenants of the Duke were summoned to appear with their termly rents. They appeared accordingly, and the factor had received ready money to the amount of about £300, when Rob Roy entered the room at the head of an armed party. The steward endeavoured to protect the Duke's property by throwing the books of accounts and money into a garret, trusting they might escape notice. But the experienced freebooter was not to be baffled where such a prize was at stake.

He recovered the books and cash, placed himself calmly in the receipt of custom, examined the accounts, pocketed the money, and gave receipts on the Duke's part, saying he would hold reckoning with the Duke of Montrose out of the damages which he had sustained by his Grace's means, in which he included the losses he had suffered, as well by the burning of his house by General Cadogan, as by the later expedition against Craig-Royston. He then requested Mr. Graham to attend him; nor does it appear that he treated him with any personal violence or even rudeness, although he informed him he regarded him as a hostage, and menaced rough usage in case he should be pursued, or in danger of being overtaken. Few more audacious feats have been performed. After some rapid changes of place, (the fatigue attending which was the only annoyance that Mr. Graham seems to have complained of,) he carried his prisoner to an island on Loch Katrine, and caused him to write to the Duke, to state that his ransom was fixed at 3,400 merks, being the balance which MacGregor pretended remained due to him, after deducting all that he owed to the Duke of Montrose.

However, after detaining Mr. Graham five or six days in custody on the island, which is still called Rob Roy's Prison, and could be no comfortable dwelling for November nights, the Outlaw seems to have despaired of attaining further advantage from his bold attempt, and suffered his prisoner to depart uninjured, with the account-books, and bills granted by the tenants, taking especial care to retain the cash.*

Other pranks are told of Rob, which argue the same boldness and sagacity as the seizure of Killearn. The Duke of Montrose, weary of his insolence, procured a quantity of arms, and distributed them among his tenantry, in order that they might defend themselves against future violences. But they fell into different hands from those they were intended for. The Mac-Gregors made separate attacks on the houses of the tenants, and disarmed them all one after another, not, as was supposed, without the consent of many of the persons so disarmed.

As a great part of the Duke's rents were payable in kind, there were girnels (granaries) established for storing up the corn at Moulin, and elsewhere on the Buchanan estate. To these storehouses Rob Roy used to repair with a sufficient force, and of course when he was least expected, and insist upon the delivery of quantities of grain, sometimes for his own use, and sometimes for the assistance of the country people, always giving regular receipts in his own name, and pretending to reckon with the Duke for what sums he received.

* The reader will find two original letters of the Duke of Montrose, with that which Mr. Graham of Killearn dispatched from his prison-house by the Outlaw's command, in the Appendix, No. II.

CHAPTER VI.

The Garrison at Inversnaid—Rob Roy as a Black-Mailer—Description of Black-Mail—A Cattle-stealing story—Rob captured by the Duke—And his escape.

In the meanwhile a garrison was established by government, the ruins of which may be still seen about half way betwixt Loch Lomond and Loch Katrine, upon Rob Roy's original property of Inversnaid. Even this military establishment could not bridle the restless MacGregor. He contrived to surprise the little fort, disarm the soldiers, and destroy the fortification. It was afterwards re-established and again taken by the MacGregors under Rob Roy's nephew, Ghlune Dhu, previous to the insurrection of 1745-6. Finally, the fort of Inversnaid was a third time repaired after the extinction of civil discord; and when we find the celebrated General Wolfe commanding in it, the imagination is strongly affected by the variety of time and events which the circumstance brings simultaneously to recollection. It is now totally dismantled. About 1792, when the author chanced to pass that way while on a tour through the Highlands, a garrison, consisting of a single veteran, was still maintained at Inversnaid. The venerable warder was reaping his barley croft in all peace and tranquillity; and when we asked admittance to repose ourselves, he

told us we would find the key of *The Fort* under the
door.

It was not strictly speaking, as a professed depre-
dator that Rob Roy now conducted his operations, but
as a sort of contractor for the police; in Scottish phrase
a lifter of black-mail.   The nature of this contract has
been described in the Novel of Waverley, and in the
notes on that work.   Mr. Graham of Gartmore's
description of the character may be here transcribed.

"The confusion and disorders of the country were so
great, and the government so absolutely neglected it,
that the sober people there were obliged to purchase
some security to their effects by shameful and igno-
minious contracts of *black-mail*. A person who had the
greatest correspondence with the thieves was agreed
with to preserve the lands contracted for from thefts,
for certain sums to be paid yearly.   Upon this fund he
employed one half of the thieves to recover stolen
cattle, and the other half of them to steal, in order to
make this agreement and black-mail contract necessary.
The estates of those gentleman who refused to contract, or give countenance to that pernicious practice,
are plundered by the thieving part of the watch, in
order to force them to purchase their protection. Their
leader calls himself the *Captain* of the *Watch*, and his
banditti go by that name.   And as this gives them a
kind of authority to traverse the country, so it makes
them capable of any mischief.   These corps through
the Highlands make altogether a very considerable

body of men, inured from their infancy to the greatest fatigues, and very capable to act in a military way when occasion offers.

" People who are ignorant and enthusiastic, who are in absolute dependence upon their chief or landlord, who are directed in their consciences by Roman Catholic priests, or non-juring clergymen, and who are not masters of any property, may easily be formed into any mould. They fear no dangers, as they have nothing to lose, and so can with ease be induced to attempt any thing. Nothing can make their condition worse; confusions and troubles do commonly indulge them in such licentiousness, that by these they better it."*

As the practice of contracting for blackmail was an obvious encouragement to rapine, and a great obstacle to the course of justice, it was, by the statute 1567, chap. 21, declared a capital crime, both on the part of him who levied and him who paid this sort of tax. But the necessity of the case prevented the execution of this severe law, I believe, in any one instance; and men went on submitting to a certain unlawful imposition rather than run the risk of utter ruin,—just as it is now found difficult or impossible to prevent those who have lost a very large sum of money by robbery, from compounding with the felons for restoration of a part of their booty.

* Letters from the North of Scotland, Vol. II., pp. 344-5.

At what rate Rob Roy levied black-mail, I never heard stated ; but there is a formal contract by which his nephew, in 1741, agreed with various landholders of estates in the counties of Perth, Stirling, and Dumbarton, to recover cattle stolen from them, or to pay the value within six months of the loss being intimated, if such intimation were made to him with sufficient dispatch, in consideration of a payment of L.5 on each L.100 of valued rent, which was not a very heavy insurance. Petty thefts were not included in the contract ; but the theft of one horse, or one head of black cattle, or of sheep exceeding the number of six, fell under the agreement.

Rob Roy's profits upon such contracts brought him in a considerable revenue in money or cattle, of which he made a popular use ; for he was publicly liberal, as well as privately beneficent. The minister of the parish of Balquhidder, whose name was Robinson, was at one time threatening to pursue the parish for an augmentation of his stipend. Rob Roy took an opportunity to assure him that he would do well to abstain from this new exaction,—a hint which the minister did not fail to understand. But to make him some indemnification, MacGregor presented him every year with a cow and a fat sheep ; and no scruples as to the mode in which the donor came by them, are said to have affected the reverend gentleman's conscience.

The following account of the proceedings of Rob Roy, on an application to him from one of his contractors, had in it something very interesting to me, as told by an old countryman in the Lennox who was present on the expedition. But as there is no point or marked incident in the story, and as it must necessarily be without the half-frightened, half-bewildered look with which the narrator accompanied his recollections, it may possibly lose its effect when transferred to paper.

My informant stated himself to have been a lad of fifteen, living with his father on the estate of a gentleman in the Lennox, whose name I have forgotten, in the capacity of herd. On a fine morning in the end of October, the period when such calamities were almost always to be apprehended, they found the Highland thieves had been down upon them, and swept away ten or twelve head of cattle. Rob Roy was sent for, and came with a party of seven or eight armed men. He heard with great gravity all that could be told him of the circumstances of the *creagh*, and expressed his confidence that the *herd-widdiefows* * could not have carried their booty far, and that he should be able to recover them. He desired that two Lowlanders should be sent on the party, as it was not to be expected that any of his gentlemen would take the trouble of driving the cattle when he should recover possession of them. My informant and his father were dispatched on the expedition. They had no good-will to the journey : nevertheless, provided with a little food, and with a

* Mad herdsmen, a name given to cattle-stealers.

dog to help them to manage the cattle, they set off with MacGregor. They travelled a long day's journey in the direction of the mountain Benvoirlich, and slept for the night in a ruinous hut or bothy. The next morning they resumed their journey among the hills, Rob Roy directing their course by signs and marks on the heath, which my informant did not understand.

About noon, Rob commanded the armed party to halt, and to lie couched in the heather where it was thickest.

" Do you and your son," he said to the oldest Lowlander, " go boldly over the hill. You will see beneath you, in a glen on the other side, your master's cattle feeding, it may be, with others; gather your own together, taking care to disturb no one else, and drive them to this place. If any one speak to, or threaten you, tell them that I am here, at the head of twenty men."

" But what if they abuse us, or kill us ? " said the Lowland peasant, by no means delighted at finding the embassy imposed on him and his son.

" If they do you any wrong," said Rob, " I will never forgive them as long as I live."

The Lowlander was by no means content with this security, but did not think it safe to dispute Rob's injunctions.

He and his son climbed the hill, therefore, found a deep valley, where there grazed, as Rob had predicted, a large herd of cattle. They cautiously selected those

which their master had lost, and took measures to drive
them over the hill. As soon as they began to remove
them, they were surprised by hearing cries and screams;
and looking around in fear and trembling, they saw a
woman, seeming to have started out of the earth, who
flyted at them, that is, scolded them, in Gaelic. When
they contrived, however, in the best Gaelic they could
muster, to deliver the message Rob Roy told them, she
became silent, and disappeared without offering them
any further annoyance. The chief heard their story on
their return, and spoke with great complacency of the
art which he possessed of putting such things to rights
without any unpleasant bustle. The party were now
on their road home, and the danger, though not the
fatigue, of the expedition was at an end.

They drove on the cattle with little repose until it
was nearly dark, when Rob proposed to halt for the
night upon a wide moor, across which a cold north-
east wind, with frost on its wing, was whistling to the
tune of the Pipers of Strath-Dearn,—the winds which
sweep a wild glen in Badenoch are so called. The
Highlanders, sheltered by their plaids, lay down in the
heath comfortably enough, but the Lowlanders had no
protection whatever. Rob Roy observing this, directed
one of his followers to afford the old man a portion of
his plaid.

"For the callant (boy), he may," said the freebooter,
"keep himself warm by walking about and watching
the cattle."

My informant heard this sentence with no small distress ; and as the frosty wind grew more and more cutting, it seemed to freeze the very blood in his young veins. He had been exposed to weather all his life, he said, but never could forget the cold of that night ; in so much that, in the bitterness of his heart, he cursed the bright moon for giving no heat with so much light. At length the sense of cold and weariness became so intolerable, that he resolved to desert his watch to seek some repose and shelter. With that purpose, he couched himself down behind one of the most bulky of the Highlanders, who acted as lieutenant to the party. Not satisfied with having secured the shelter of the man's large person, he coveted a share of his plaid, and by imperceptible degrees drew a corner of it round him. He was now comparatively in paradise, and slept sound till daybreak, when he awoke, and was terribly afraid on observing that his nocturnal operations had altogether uncovered the dhuinie-wassell's neck and shoulders, which, lacking the plaid which should have protected them, were covered with *cranreuch* (*i.e.* hoar frost). The lad rose in great dread of a beating, at least, when it should be found how luxuriously he had been accommodated at the expense of a principal person of the party. Good Mr. Lieutenant, however, got up and shook himself, rubbing off the hoar frost with his plaid, and muttering something of a *cauld neight.* They then drove on the cattle, which were restored to their owner without farther adventure. The above can hardly be termed a tale, but yet it contains materials both for the poet and artist.

It was perhaps about the same time that, by a rapid march into the Balquhidder hills at the head of a body of his own tenantry, the Duke of Montrose actually surprised Rob Roy, and made him prisoner. He was mounted behind one of the Duke's followers, named James Stewart, and made fast to him by a horse-girth. The person who had him thus in charge was grandfather of the intelligent man of the same name, now deceased, who lately kept the inn in the vicinity of Loch Katrine, and acted as a guide to visitors through that beautiful scenery. From him I learned the story many years before he was either a publican or a guide, except to moorfowl shooters.—It was evening, (to resume the story) and the Duke was pressing on to lodge his prisoner, so long sought after in vain, in some place of security, when in crossing the Teith or Forth, I forget which, MacGregor took an opportunity to conjure Stewart, by all the ties of old acquaintance and good-neighbourhood, to give him some chance of an escape from an assured doom. Stewart was moved with compassion, perhaps with fear. He slipped the girth-buckle, and Rob, dropping down from behind the horse's croupe, dived, swam, and escaped, pretty much as described in the novel. When James Stewart came on shore, the Duke hastily demanded where his prisoner was; and as no distinct answer was returned, instantly suspected Stewart's connivance at the escape of the outlaw ; and, drawing a steel pistol from his belt, struck him down with a blow on the head, from the effects of which, his descendant said, he never completely recovered.

In the success of his repeated escapes from the pursuit of his powerful enemy, Rob Roy at length became wanton and facetious. He wrote a mock challenge to the Duke, which he circulated among his friends to amuse them over a bottle. The reader will find this document in the Appendix.* It is written in a good hand, and not particularly deficient in grammar or spelling. Our Southern readers must be given to understand that it was a piece of humour,—a *quiz*, in short,—on the part of the outlaw, who was too sagacious to propose such a rencontre in reality. This letter was written in the year 1719.

CHAPTER VII.

Rob Roy's declaration to General Wade—Becomes more peaceable in his habits—Gives some attention to religious matters—Dispute with the Stewarts of Appin—Rob's combat with Alaster Stewart —Rob Roy's death—Estimate of his life and character—Rob's five sons—Renewal of quarrel with MacLarens and Stewarts.

In the following year Rob Roy composed another epistle, very little to his own reputation, as he therein confesses having played booty during the civil war of

* Appendix, No. III.

1715. It is addressed to General Wade, at that time
engaged in disarming the Highland clans, and making
military roads through the country. The letter is a
singular composition. It sets out the writer's real and
unfeigned desire to have offered his service to King
George, but for his liability to be thrown into jail for
a civil debt, at the instance of the Duke of Montrose.
Being thus debarred from taking the right side, he
acknowledged he embraced the wrong one, upon
Falstaff's principle, that since the King wanted men
and the rebels soldiers, it were worse shame to be idle
in such a stirring world, than to embrace the worst
side, were it as black as rebellion could make it. The
impossibility of his being neutral in such a debate, Rob
seems to lay down as an undeniable proposition. At
the same time, while he acknowledges having been
forced into an unnatural rebellion against King George,
he pleads that he not only avoided acting offensively
against his Majesty's forces on all occasions, but, on
the contrary, sent to them what intelligence he could
collect from time to time; for the truth of which he
refers to His Grace the Duke of Argyle. What influence this plea had on General Wade we have no means
of knowing.

Rob Roy appears to have continued to live very
much as usual. His fame, in the meanwhile, passed
beyond the narrow limits of the country in which he
resided. A pretended history of him appeared in
London during his lifetime, under the title of the High-

land Rogue. It is a catch-penny publication, bearing in front the effigy of a species of ogre, with a beard of a foot in length; and his actions are as much exaggerated as his personal appearance. Some few of the best known adventures of the hero are told, though with little accuracy; but the greater part of the pamphlet is entirely fictitious. It is great pity so excellent a theme for a narrative of the kind had not fallen into the hands of De Foe, who was engaged at the time on subjects somewhat similar, though inferior in dignity and interest.

As Rob Roy advanced in years he became more peaceable in his habits, and his nephew, Ghlune Dhu, with most of his tribe, renounced those peculiar quarrels with the Duke of Montrose, by which his uncle had been distinguished. The policy of that great family had latterly been rather to attach this wild tribe by kindness than to follow the mode of violence which had been hitherto ineffectually resorted to. Leases at a low rent were granted to many of the MacGregors, who had heretofore held possessions in the Duke's Highland property merely by occupancy; and Glengyle, (or Black-knee,) who continued to act as collector of black-mail, managed his police, as a commander of the Highland watch arrayed at the charge of government. He is said to have strictly abstained from the open and lawless depredations which his kinsman had practised.

It was probably after this state of temporary quiet

had been obtained, that Rob Roy began to think of the
concerns of his future state. He had been bred, and
and long professed himself, a Protestant; but in his
later years he embraced the Roman Catholic faith,—
perhaps on Mrs. Cole's principle, that it was a comfortable religion for one of his calling. He is said to have
alleged as the cause of his conversion, a desire to
gratify the noble family of Perth, who were then strict
Catholics. Having, as he observed, assumed the name
of the Duke of Argyle, his first protector, he could pay
no compliment worth the Earl of Perth's acceptance,
save complying with his mode of religion. Rob did not
pretend, when pressed closely on the subject, to justify
all the tenets of Catholicism, and acknowledged that
extreme unction always appeared to him a great waste
of *ulzie*, or oil.*

In the last years of Rob Roy's life his clan was involved in a dispute with one more powerful than themselves. Stewart of Appin, a chief of the tribe so named,
was proprietor of a hill-farm in the Braes of Balquhidder, called Invernenty. The MacGregors of Rob
Roy's tribe claimed a right to it by ancient occupancy,
and declared they would oppose to the uttermost the
settlement of any person upon the farm not being of
their own name. The Stewarts came down with two
hundred men, well armed, to do themselves justice by

* Such an admission is ascribed to the robber, Donald Bean Lean, in
Waverley, Vol. II., p. 309.

main force. The MacGregors took the field, but were
unable to muster an equal strength. Rob Roy, finding
himself the weaker party, asked a parley, in which he
represented that both clans were friends to the *King*,
and that he was unwilling they should be weakened by
mutual conflict, and thus made a merit of surrendering
to Appin the disputed territory of Invernenty. Appin,
accordingly, settled as tenants there, at an easy quit-
rent, the MacLarens, a family dependent on the
Stewarts and from whose character for strength and
bravery, it was expected that they would make their
right good if annoyed by the MacGregors. When all
this had been amicably adjusted, in presence of the two
clans drawn up in arms near the Kirk of Balquhidder,
Rob Roy, apparently fearing his tribe might be thought
to have conceded too much upon the occasion, stepped
forward and said, that where so many gallant men
were met in arms, it would be shameful to part without a trial of skill, and therefore he took the freedom
to invite any gentleman of the Stewarts present to
exchange a few blows with him for the honour of
their respective clans. The brother-in-law of Appin,
and second chieftain of the clan, Alaster Stewart of
Invernahyle, accepted the challenge, and they encountered with broadsword and target before their
respective kinsmen. Some accounts state that Appin
himself was Rob Roy's antagonist on this occasion.
My recollection, from the account of Invernahyle himself, was as stated. But the period when I received

the information is now so distant, that it is possible I
may be mistaken. Invernahyle was rather of low
stature, but very well made, athletic, and an excellent
swordsman.

The combat lasted till Rob received a slight wound
in the arm, which was the usual termination of such a
combat when fought for honour only, and not with a
mortal purpose. Rob Roy dropped his point, and con-
gratulated his adversary on having been the first man
who ever drew blood from him. The victor generously
acknowledged, that without the advantage of youth,
and the agility accompanying it, he probably could not
have come off with advantage.

This was probably one of Rob Roy's last exploits in
arms. The time of his death is not known with certainty, but he is generally said to have survived 1738,
and to have died an aged man. When he found himself approaching his final change, he expressed some
contrition for particular parts of his life. His wife
laughed at these scruples of conscience, and exhorted
him to die like a man, as he had lived. In reply, he
rebuked her for her violent passions, and the counsel
she had given him. "You have put strife," he said,
"betwixt me and the best men of the country, and
now you would place enmity between me and my God."

There is a tradition, no way inconsistent with the
former, if the character of Rob Roy be justly considered,
that while on his death-bed, he learned that a person,
with whom he was at enmity, proposed to visit him.

"Raise me from my bed," said the invalid; "throw my plaid around me, and bring me my claymore, dirk, and pistols—it shall never be said that a foeman saw Rob Roy MacGregor defenceless and unarmed."

His foeman, conjectured to be one of the MacLarens before and after mentioned, entered and paid his compliments, enquiring after the health of his formidable neighbour.   Rob Roy maintained a cold, haughty civility during their short conference, and so soon as he had left the house,—

"Now," he said, "all is over—let the piper play *Ha til mi tulidh*, (we return no more)."

And he is said to have expired before the dirge was finished.

This singular man died in bed in his own house, in the parish of Balquhidder.   He was buried in the churchyard of the same parish, where his tombstone is only distinguished by a rude attempt at the figure of a broadsword.

The character of Rob Roy is, of course, a mixed one. His sagacity, boldness, and prudence, qualities so highly necessary to success in war, became in some degree vices from the manner in which they were employed. The circumstances of his education, however, must be admitted as some extenuation of his habitual transgressions against the law; and for his political tergiversations, he might in that distracted period plead the example of men far more powerful, and less excusable in becoming the sport of circumstances, than the poor and desperate outlaw. On the other hand, he was in the constant exercise of virtues, the more meritorious as they seem inconsistent with his general character. Pursuing the occupation of a predatory chieftain,—in modern phrase, a captain of banditti,—Rob Roy was moderate in his revenge, and humane in his successes. No charge of cruelty or bloodshed, unless in battle, is brought against his memory. In like manner, the formidable outlaw was the friend of the poor, and, to the utmost of his ability, the support of the widow and the orphan—kept his word when pledged—and died lamented in his own wild country, where there were hearts grateful for his beneficence, though their minds were not sufficiently instructed to appreciate his errors.

The author perhaps ought to stop here; but the fate of a part of Rob Roy's family was so extraordinary, as to call for a continuation of this somewhat prolix account, as affording an interesting chapter, not on Highland manners alone, but on every stage of society in which people of a primitive and half-civilized tribe are brought into close contact with a nation, in which civilization and polity has attained a complete superiority.

Rob had five sons,—Coll, Ronald, James, Duncan, and Robert. Nothing occurs worth notice concerning three of them ; but James, who was a very handsome man, seems to have had a good deal of his father's spirit, and the mantle of Dougal Ciar Mohr had apparently descended on the shoulders of Robin Oig, that is, young Robin. Shortly after Rob Roy's death, the ill-will which the MacGregors entertained against the MacLarens again broke out, at the instigation, it was said, of Rob's widow, who seems thus far to have deserved the character given to her by her husband, as an Até stirring up to blood and strife. Robin Oig, under her instigation, swore that as soon as he could get back a certain gun which had belonged to his father, and had been lately at Doune to be repaired, he would shoot MacLaren, for having presumed to settle on his mother's land. This fatal piece was taken from Robin Oig, when he was seized many years afterwards. It remained in possession of the magistrates, before whom he was brought for examination, and now makes part of a small collection of arms belonging to the author. It is a Spanish-barrelled gun, marked with the letters R. M. C. for Robert MacGregor Campbell. He was as good as his word, and shot MacLaren when between the stilts of his plough, wounding him mortally.

The aid of a Highland leech was procured, who probed the wound with a probe made out of a castock, *i. e.* the stalk of a cole-wort or cabbage. This learned gentleman declared he would not venture to prescribe, not knowing with what shot the patient had been wounded. MacLaren died, and about the same time his cattle were houghed and his live stock destroyed in a barbarous manner.

Robin Oig, after this feat—which one of his bio-

graphers represents as the unhappy discharge of a gun—
retired to his mother's house, to boast that he had
drawn the first blood in the quarrel aforesaid. On the
approach of troops, and a body of the Stewarts, who
were bound to take up the cause of their tenant, Robin
Oig absconded, and escaped all search.

The doctor already mentioned, by name Callam
MacInleister, with James and Ronald, brothers to the
actual perpetrator of the murder, were brought to trial.
But as they contrived to represent the action as a rash
deed committed by the " daft callant Rob," to which
they were not accessary, the jury found their accession
to the crime was Not Proven. The alleged acts of
spoil and violence on the MacLarens' cattle were also
found to be unsupported by evidence. As it was
proved, however, that the two brothers, Ronald and
James, were held and reputed thieves, they were
appointed to find caution to the extent of £200, for
their good behaviour for seven years.

The author is uncertain whether it is worth while to
mention that he had a personal opportunity of observing, even in his own time, that the king's writ did not
pass quite current in the Braes of Balquhidder. There
were very considerable debts due by Stewart of Appin
(chiefly to the author's family), which were likely to be
lost to the creditors, if they could not be made avail-
able out of this same farm of Inverenty, the scene of
the murder done upon MacLaren.

His family, consisting of several strapping deerstalkers, still possessed the farm, by virtue of a long lease, for a trifling rent. There was no chance of any one buying it with such an encumbrance, and a transaction was entered into by the MacLarens, who, being desirous to emigrate to America, agreed to sell their lease to the creditors for £500, and to remove at the next term of Whitsunday. But whether they repented their bargain, or desired to make a better, or whether from a mere point of honour, the MacLarens declared they would not permit a summons of removal to be executed against them, which was necessary for the legal completion of the bargain. And such was the general impression that they were men capable of resisting the legal execution of warning by very effectual means, no king's messenger would execute the summons without the support of a military force. An escort of a sergeant and six men was obtained from a Highland regiment lying in Stirling; and the author, then a writer's apprentice, equivalent to the honourable situation of an attorney's clerk, was invested with the superintendence of the expedition, with directions to see that the messenger discharged his duty fully, and that the gallant sergeant did not exceed his part by committing violence or plunder. And thus it happened, oddly enough, that the author first entered the romantic scenery of Loch Katrine, of which he may perhaps say he has somewhat extended the reputation, riding in all the dignity of danger, with a front and rear guard, and loaded arms. The sergeant was absolutely a Highland Sergeant Kite, full of stories of Rob Roy and of himself, and a very good companion. We experienced no interruption whatever, and when we came to Invernenty, found the house deserted. We took up our quarters for the night, and used some of the victuals which we found there. On the morning we returned as unmolested as we came.

The MacLarens, who probably never thought of any serious opposition, received their money, and went to America, where, having had some slight share in removing them from their *pauvera regna,* I sincerely hope they prospered.

The rent of Invernenty instantly rose from £10 to £70 or £80; and when sold, the farm was purchased (I think by the late laird of MacNab) at a price higher in proportion than what even the modern rent authorised the parties interested to hope for.

The spirit of clanship was at that time so strong—to which must be added the wish to secure the adherence of stout, able-bodied, and, as the Scotch phrase then went, *pretty* men—that the representative of the noble family of Perth condescended to act openly as patron of the MacGregors, and appeared as such upon their trial. So at least the author was informed by the late Robert MacIntosh, Esq., advocate. The circumstance may, however, have occurred later than 1736, the year in which this first trial took place.

Robin Oig served for a time in the 42d regiment, and was present at the battle of Fontenoy, where he was made prisoner and wounded. He was exchanged, returned to Scotland, and obtained his discharge. He afterwards appeared openly in the MacGregor's country; and, notwithstanding his outlawry, married a daughter of Graham of Drunkie, a gentleman of some property. His wife died a few years afterwards.

CHAPTER VIII.

The MacGregors in the Rising of 1845—At the Battle of Prestonpans —At the Battle of Culloden—Return home—The Matrimonial Tragedy—The Story of the Abduction—Liberation of Jean Keay —Her Decease.

THE insurrection of 1745 soon afterwards called the MacGregors to arms. Robert MacGregor of Glencarnoch, generally regarded as the chief of the whole name, and grandfather of Sir John, whom the clan received in that character, raised a MacGregor regiment, with which he joined the standard of the Chevalier. The race of Ciar Mohr, however, affecting independence and commanded by Glengyle and his cousin James Roy MacGregor, did not join this kindred corps, but united themselves to the levies of the titular Duke of Perth, until William MacGregor Drummond of Bolhaldin, whom they regarded as head of their branch of Clan-Alpine, should come over from France. To cement the union after the Highland fashion, James laid down the name of Campbell and assumed that of Drummond, in compliment to Lord Perth. He was also called James Roy, after his father, and James Mohr, or Big James, from his height. His corps, the relics of his father Rob's band, behaved with great activity; with only twelve men he succeeded in surprising and burning, for the second time, the fort at Inversnaid, constructed for the express purpose of bridling the country of the MacGregors.

What rank or command James MacGregor had, is uncertain. He calls himself Major, and Chevalier Johnstone calls him Captain. He must have held rank under Ghlune Dhu, his kinsman, but his active and audacious character placed him above the rest of his brethren. Many of his followers were unarmed; he supplied the want of guns and swords with scythe-blades set straight upon their handles.

At the battle of Prestonpans, James Roy distinguished himself. "His company," says Chevalier Johnstone, "did great execution with their scythes." They cut the legs of the horses in two; the riders through the middle of their bodies. MacGregor was brave and intrepid, but, at the same time, somewhat whimsical and singular. When advancing to the charge with his company, he received five wounds, two of them from balls that pierced his body through and through. Stretched on the ground, with his head resting on his hand, he called out loudly to the Highlanders of his company,—

"My lads, I am not dead. By G—, I shall see if any of you does not do his duty."

The victory, as is well known, was instantly obtained.

In some curious letters of James Roy,* it appears that his thigh bone was broken on this occasion, and that he, nevertheless, rejoined the army with six companies, and was present at the battle of Culloden. After that defeat the Clan MacGregor kept together in a body, and did not disperse till they had returned into their own country. They brought James Roy with them in a litter: and, without being particularly molested, he was permitted to reside in the MacGregor's country along with his brothers.

James MacGregor Drummond was attainted for high treason with persons of more importance. But it appears he had entered into some communication with government, as, in the letters quoted, he mentions having obtained a pass from the Lord Justice Clerk in 1747, which was a sufficient protection to him from the military. The circumstance is obscurely stated in one of the letters already quoted, but may perhaps, joined to subsequent incidents, authorise the suspicion that James, like his father, could look at both sides of the cards. As the confusion of the country subsided, the MacGregors, like foxes which had baffled the hounds, drew back to their old haunts, and lived un-

* Published in Blackwood's Magazine, Vol. II., p. 228.

molested.   But an atrocious outrage, in which the sons
of Rob Roy were concerned, brought at length on the
family the full vengeance of the law.

James Roy was a married man, and had fourteen
children.   But his brother, Robin Oig, was now a
widower; and it was resolved, if possible, that he
should make his fortune by carrying off and marrying,
by force if necessary, some woman of fortune from the
Lowlands.

The imagination of the half-civilized Highlanders
was less shocked at the idea of this particular species
of violence, than might be expected from their general
kindness to the weaker sex when they make part
of their own families.   But all their views were
tinged with the idea that they lived in a state of
war; and in such a state, from the time of the siege
of Troy to " the moment when Previsa fell,"* the female
captives are, to uncivilized victors, the most valuable
part of the booty.

"The wealthy are slaughter'd, the lovely are spared."

We need not refer to the rape of the Sabines, or to a
similar instance in the Book of Judges, for evidence
that such deeds of violence have been committed upon
a large scale.   Indeed, this sort of enterprise was so
common along the Highland line as to give rise to a
variety of songs and ballads.†   The annals of Ireland,

* Childe Harold's Pilgrimage, Canto II.
† See Appendix, No. V.

as well as those of Scotland, prove the crime to have
been common in the more lawless parts of both countries; and any woman who happened to please a man
of spirit who came of a good house, and possessed a
few chosen friends, and a retreat in the mountains, was
not permitted the alternative of saying him nay. What
is more, it would seem that the women themselves,
most interested in the immunities of their sex, were,
among the lower classes, accustomed to regard such
marriages as that which is presently to be detailed as
"pretty Fanny's way," or rather, the way of Donald
with pretty Fanny.   It is not a great many years
since a respectable woman, above the lower rank
of life, expressed herself very warmly to the author
on his taking the freedom to censure the behaviour
of the MacGregors on the occasion in question. She
said—

"That there was no use in giving a bride too much
choice upon such occasions : that the marriages were
the happiest lang syne which had been done off hand."

Finally, she averred that her "own mother had
never seen her father till the night he brought her up
from the Lennox, with ten head of black cattle, and
there had not been a happier family in the country."

James Drummond and his brethren having similar
opinions with the author's old acquaintance, and
debating how they might raise the fallen fortunes of
their clan, formed a resolution to settle their brother's

fortune by striking up an advantageous marriage
betwixt Robin Oig and one Jean Key, or Wright, a
young woman scarce twenty years old, and who had
been left about two months a widow by the death of
her husband. Her property was estimated at only from
16,000 to 18,000 merks, but it seems to have been sufficient temptation to these men to join in the commission of a great crime.

This poor young victim lived with her mother in her
own house at Edinbilly, in the parish of Balfron and
shire of Stirling. At this place, in the night of 3d
December 1750, the sons of Rob Roy, and particularly
James Mohr and Robin Oig, rushed into the house
where the object of their attack was resident, presented
guns, swords, and pistols to the males of the family,
and terrified the women by threatening to break open
the doors if Jean Key was not surrendered, as, said
James Roy, "his brother was a young fellow determined to make his fortune." Having, at length,
dragged the object of their lawless purpose from
her place of concealment, they tore her from her
mother's arms, mounted her on a horse before one of
the gang, and carried her off in spite of her screams
and cries, which were long heard after the terrified
spectators of the outrage could no longer see the party
retreat through the darkness. In her attempts to
escape, the poor young woman threw herself from the
horse on which they had placed her, and in so doing
wrenched her side. They then laid her double over

the pummel of the saddle, and transported her through the mosses and moors till the pain of the injury she had suffered in her side, augmented by the uneasiness of her posture, made her consent to sit upright.

In the execution of this crime they stopped at more houses than one, but none of the inhabitants dared interrupt their proceedings. Amongst others who saw them was that classical and accomplished scholar the late Professor William Richardson of Glasgow, who used to describe as a terrible dream their violent and noisy entrance into the house where he was then residing. The Highlanders filled the little kitchen, brandishing their arms, demanding what they pleased, and receiving whatever they demanded. James Mohr, he said, was a tall, stern, and soldier-like man. Robin Oig looked more gentle; dark, but yet ruddy in complexion —a good-looking young savage. The victim was so dishevelled in her dress, and forlorn in her appearance and demeanour, that he could hardly tell whether she was alive or dead.

The gang carried the unfortunate woman to Rowerdennan, where they had a priest unscrupulous enough to read the marriage service, while James Mohr forcibly held the bride up before him; and the priest declared the couple man and wife, even while she protested against the infamy of his conduct. Under the same threats of violence, which had been all along used to enforce their scheme, the poor victim was compelled to reside with the pretended husband who was thus forced upon her. They even dared to carry her to the public church of Balquhidder, where the officiating clergyman (the same who had been Rob Roy's pensioner) only asked them if they were married persons. Robert MacGregor answered in the affirmative; the terrified female was silent.

The country was now too effectually subjected to the law for this vile outrage to be followed by the advantages proposed by the actors. Military parties were sent out in every direction to seize the Mac-Gregors, who were for two or three weeks compelled to shift from one place to another in the mountains, bearing the unfortunate Jean Key along with them. In the mean while, the Supreme Civil Court issued a warrant sequestrating the property of Jean Key, or Wright, which removed out of the reach of the actors in the violence the prize which they expected. They had, however, adopted a belief of the poor woman's spirit being so far broken that she would prefer submitting to her condition, and adhering to Robert Oig as her husband, rather than incur the disgrace of appearing in such a cause in an open court. It was, indeed, a delicate experiment, but their kinsman Glengyle, chief of their immediate family, was of a temper averse to lawless proceedings. Such, at least, was his general character; for when James Mohr, while perpetrating the violence at Edinbilly, called out, in order to overawe opposition, that Glengyle was lying in the moor with a hundred men to patronise his enterprise, Jean Key told him he lied, since she was confident Glengyle would never countenance so scoundrelly a business. And the captive's friends having had recourse to his advice, they feared that he would withdraw his protection if they refused to place the prisoner at liberty.

The brethren resolved therefore to liberate the unhappy woman, but previously had recourse to every measure which should oblige her, either from fear or otherwise, to own her marriage with Robin Oig. The cailliachs (old Highland hags) administered drugs, which were designed to have the effect of philtres, but were probably deleterious. James Mohr at one time threatened that if she did not acquiesce in the match she would find that there were enough of men in the Highlands to bring the heads of two of her uncles who were pursuing the civil lawsuit. At another time he fell down on his knees, and confessed he had been accessory to wronging her, but begged she would not ruin his innocent wife and large family. She was made to swear she would not prosecute the brethren for the offence they had committed; and she was obliged, by threats, to subscribe papers which were tendered to her, intimating that she was carried off in consequence of her own previous request.

James Mohr Drummond accordingly brought his pretended sister-in-law to Edinburgh, where, for some little time, she was carried about from one house to another, watched by those with whom she was lodged, and never permitted to go out alone or even to approach the window. The Court of Session, considering the peculiarity of the case, and regarding Jean Key as being still under some forcible restraint, took her person under their own special charge, and appointed her to reside in the family of Mr. Wightman of Mauldsley, a gentleman of respectability, who was married to one of her near relatives. Two sentinels kept guard on the house day and night—a precaution not deemed superfluous when the MacGregors were in question. She was allowed to go out whenever she chose, and to see whomsoever she had a mind, as well as the men of law employed in the civil suit on either side. When she first came to Mr. Wightman's house, she seemed broken down with affright and suffering, so changed in features that her mother hardly knew her, and so shaken in mind that she scarce could recognise her parent. It was long before she could be assured that she was in perfect safety. But when she at length received confidence in her situation, she made a judicial declaration or affidavit, telling the full history of her wrongs, imputing to fear her former silence on the subject, and expressing her resolution not to prosecute those who had injured her, in respect of the oath which she had been compelled to take. From the possible breach of such an oath, though a compulsory one, she was relieved by the forms of Scottish jurisprudence, in that respect more equitable than those of England, prosecutions for crimes being always conducted at the expense and charge of the King, without inconvenience or cost to the private party who has sustained the wrong.   But the unhappy sufferer did not live to be either accuser or witness against those who had so deeply injured her.

James Mohr Drummond had left Edinburgh so soon as his half-dead prey had been taken from his clutches. Mrs. Key, or Wright, was released from her species of confinement there, and removed to Glasgow, under the escort of Mr. Wightman.   As they passed the Hill of Shotts, her escort chanced to say,

"This is a very wild spot; what if the MacGregors should come upon us?"

"God forbid!" was her immediate answer, "the very sight of them would kill me."

She continued to reside at Glasgow, without venturing to return to her own house at Edinbilly.   Her pretended husband made some attempts to obtain an interview with her, which she steadily rejected.   She died on the 4th October, 1751.   The information for the crown hints that her decease might be the consequence of the usage she received.   But there is a general report that she died of the small-pox.

CHAPTER IX.

The Trial—James Mohr MacGregor's imprisonment and romantic
escape—Outlawed—A remarkable Highland Story—James's later
days and death—Robert Oig MacGregor's Trial and Execution.

IN the meantime, James Mohr, or Drummond, fell into
the hands of justice.   He was considered as the insti-
gator of the whole affair.   Nay, the deceased had
informed her friends that, on the night of her being
carried off, Robin Oig, moved by her cries and tears,
had partly consented to let her return, when James
came up, with a pistol in his hand, and, asking whether
he was such a coward as to relinquish an enterprise in
which he had risked every thing to procure him a
fortune, in a manner compelled his brother to persevere.
James's trial took place on 13th July, 1752, and was
conducted with the utmost fairness and impartiality.
Several witnesses, all of the MacGregor family, swore
that the marriage was performed with every appearance
of acquiescence on the woman's part; and three or four
witnesses, one of them sheriff-substitute of the county,
swore she might have made her escape if she wished,
and the magistrate stated that he offered her assistance
if she felt desirous to do so.   But when asked why he,
in his official capacity, did not arrest the MacGregors,
he could only answer, that he had not force sufficient
to make the attempt.

The judicial declarations of Jean Key, or Wright,

stated the violent manner in which she had been
carried off, and they were confirmed by many of her
friends, from her private communications with them,
which the event of her death rendered good evidence.
Indeed, the fact of her abduction (to use a Scottish
law term) was completely proved by impartial witnesses. The unhappy woman admitted that she had
pretended'acquiescence in her fate on several occasions,
because she dared not trust such as offered to assist her
to escape, not even the sheriff-substitute.

The jury brought in a special verdict, finding that
Jean Key, or Wright, had been forcibly carried off from
her house, as charged in the indictment, and that the
accused had failed to show that she was herself privy
and consenting to this act of outrage. But they found
the forcible marriage, and subsequent violence, was not
proved ; and also found, in alleviation of the panel's
guilt in the premises, that Jean Key did afterwards acquiesce in her condition. Eleven of the jury, using the
names of other four who were absent, subscribed a
letter to the Court, stating it was their purpose and desire, by such special verdict, to take the panel's case
out of the class of capital crimes.

Learned informations (written arguments) on the
import of the verdict, which must be allowed a very
mild one in the circumstances, were laid before the
High Court of Justiciary. This point is very learnedly
debated in these pleadings by Mr. Grant, Solicitor for
the Crown, and the celebrated Mr. Lockhart, on the

part of the prisoner ; but James Mohr did not wait the event of the Court's decision.

He had been committed to the Castle of Edinburgh on some reports that an escape would be attempted. Yet he contrived to achieve his liberty even from that fortress.   His daughter had the address to enter the prison, disguised as a cobbler, bringing home work as she pretended.   In this cobbler's dress her father quickly arrayed himself.   The wife and daughter of the prisoner were heard by the sentinels scolding the supposed cobbler for having done his work ill, and the man came out with his hat slouched over his eyes, and grumbling, as if at the manner in which they had treated him.   In this way the prisoner passed all the guards without suspicion, and made his escape to France.   He was afterwards outlawed by the Court of Justiciary, which proceeded to the trial of Duncan MacGregor, or Drummond, his brother, 15th January, 1753.   The accused had unquestionably been with the party which carried off Jean Key ; but no evidence being brought which applied to him individually and directly, the jury found him not guilty, and nothing more is known of his fate.

That of James MacGregor, who, from talent and activity, if not by seniority, may be considered as head of the family, has been long misrepresented, as it has been generally averred in Law Reports, as well as elsewhere, that his outlawry was reversed, and that he returned and died in Scotland.   But the curious letters published in *Blackwood's Magazine* for December, 1817, show this to be an error. The first of these documents is a petition to Charles Edward. It is dated 20th September, 1753, and pleads his service to the cause of the Stewarts, ascribing his exile to the persecution of the Hanoverian Government, without any allusion to the affair of Jean Key, or the Court of Justiciary. It is stated to be forwarded by MacGregor Drummond of Bohaldie, whom, as before mentioned, James Mohr acknowledged as his chief.

The effect which this petition produced does not appear. Some temporary relief was perhaps obtained. But, soon after, this daring adventurer was engaged in a very dark intrigue against an exile of his own country, and placed pretty nearly in his own circumstances. A remarkable Highland story must be here briefly alluded to. Mr. Campbell of Glenure, who had been named factor for Government on the forfeited estates of Stewart of Ardshiel, was shot dead by an assassin as he passed through the wood of Lettermore, after crossing the ferry of Ballichulish. A gentleman, named James Stewart, a natural brother of Ardshiel the forfeited person, was tried as being accessory to the murder, and condemned and executed upon very doubtful evidence; the heaviest part of which only amounted to the accused person having assisted a nephew of his own, called Allan Breck Stewart, with money to escape after the deed was done. Not satisfied with this vengeance, which was obtained in a manner little to the honour of the dispensation of justice at the time, the friends of the deceased Glenure were eagerly desirous to obtain possession of the person of Allan Breck Stewart, supposed to be the actual homicide. James Mohr Drummond was secretly applied to to trepan Stewart to the sea-coast, and bring him over to Britain to almost certain death.

Drummond MacGregor had kindred connexions with the slain Glenure ; and, besides, the MacGregors and Campbells had been friends of late, while the former clan and the Stewarts had, as we have seen, been recently at feud ; lastly, Robert Oig was now in custody at Edinburgh, and James was desirous to do some service by which his brother might be saved. The joint force of these motives may, in James's estimation of right and wrong, have been some vindication for engaging in such an enterprise, although, as must be necessarily supposed, it could only be executed by treachery of a gross description. MacGregor stipulated for a license to return to England, promising to bring Allan Breck thither along with him. But the intended victim was put upon his guard by two countrymen, who suspected James's intentions towards him. He escaped from his kidnapper, after, as MacGregor alleged, robbing his portmanteau of some clothes and four snuffboxes. Such a charge, it may be observed, could scarce have been made unless the parties had been living on a footing of intimacy, and had access to each other's baggage.

Although James Drummond had thus missed his blow in the matter of Allan Breck Stewart, he used his license to make a journey to London, and had an interview, as he avers, with Lord Holdernesse. His Lordship, and the Under-Secretary, put many puzzling questions to him; and, as he says, offered him a situation, which would bring him bread, in the Government's service. This office was advantageous as to emolument; but in the opinion of James Drummond, his acceptance of it would have been a disgrace to his birth, and have rendered him a scourge to his country. If such a tempting offer and sturdy rejection had any foundation in fact, it probably relates to some plan of espionage on the Jacobites, which the Government might hope to carry on by means of a man who, in the matter of Allan Breck Stewart, had shown no great nicety of feeling. Drummond MacGregor was so far accommodating as to intimate his willingness to act in any station in which other gentlemen of honour served, but not otherwise; an answer which, compared with some passages of his past life, may remind the reader of Ancient Pistol standing upon his reputation.

Having thus proved intractable, as he tells the story, to the proposals of Lord Holdernesse, James Drummond was ordered instantly to quit England.

On his return to France his condition seems to have been utterly disastrous. He was seized with fever and gravel, ill consequently in body, and weakened and dispirited in mind. Allan Breck Stewart threatened to

put him to death in revenge of the designs he had
harboured against him. Allan Breck Stewart was a
man likely in such a matter to keep his word. James
Drummond MacGregor and he, like Katherine and
Petruchio, were well matched "for a couple of quiet
ones." Allan Breck lived till the beginning of the
French Revolution. About 1789, a friend of mine, then
residing at Paris, was invited to see some procession
which was supposed likely to interest him, from the
windows of an apartment occupied by a Scottish
Benedictine priest. He found, sitting by the fire, a
tall, thin, raw-boned, grim-looking old man, with the
petit croix of St. Louis. His visage was strongly
marked by the irregular projections of the cheek-bones
and chin. His eyes were grey. His grizzled hair exhibited marks of having been red, and his complexion
was weather-beaten, and remarkably freckled. Some
civilities in French passed between the old man and
my friend, in the course of which they talked of the
streets and squares of Paris, till at length the old
soldier, for such he seemed, and such he was, said with
a sigh, in a sharp Highland accent,

" Deil ane o' them a' is worth the Hie street of
Edinburgh ! "

On enquiry, this admirer of Auld Reekie, which he
was never to see again, proved to be Allan Breck
Stewart. He lived decently on his little pension, and
had, in no subsequent period of his life, shown any
thing of the savage mood, in which he is generally

believed to have assassinated the enemy and oppressor, as he supposed him, of his family and clan.

The Stewart clan were in the highest degree unfriendly to him : and his late expedition to London had been attended with many suspicious circumstances, amongst which it was not the slightest that he had kept his purpose secret from his chief Bohaldie. His intercourse with Lord Holdernesse was suspicious. The Jacobites were probably, like Don Bernard de Castel Blazo, in Gil Blas, little disposed to like those who kept company with Alguazils.   MacDonnell of Lochgarry, a man of unquestioned honour, lodged an information against James Drummond before the High Bailie of Dunkirk, accusing him of being a spy, so that he found himself obliged to leave that town and come to Paris, with only the sum of thirteen livres for his immediate subsistence, and with absolute beggary staring him in the face.

We do not offer the convicted common thief, the accomplice in MacLaren's assassination, or the manager of the outrage against Jean Key, as an object of sympathy : but it is melancholy to look on the dying struggles even of a wolf or tiger, creatures of a species directly hostile to our own ; and, in like manner, the utter distress of this man, whose faults may have sprung from a wild system of education, working on a haughty temper, will not be perused without some pity. In his last letter to Bohaldie, dated Paris, 25th September, 1754, he describes his state of destitution as absolute, and expresses himself willing to exercise his talents in breaking or breeding horses, or as a hunter or fowler, if he could only procure employment in such an inferior capacity till something better should occur. An Englishman may smile, but a Scotsman will sigh at the postscript, in which the poor starving exile asks the loan of his patron's bagpipes that he might play over some of the melancholy tunes of his own land. But the effect of music arises, in a great degree, from association, and sounds which might jar the nerves of a Londoner or Parisian, bring back to the Highlander his lofty mountain, wild lake, and the deeds of his fathers of the glen. To prove MacGregor's claim to our reader's compassion, we here insert the last part of the letter alluded to.

" By all appearance I am born to suffer crosses, and it seems they're not at an end, for such is my wretched case at present, that I do not know earthly where to go or what to do, as I have no subsistence to keep body and soul together. All that I have carried here is about 13 livres, and have taken a room at my old quarters in Hotel St. Pierre, Rue de Cordier. I send you the bearer, begging of you to let me know if you are to be in town soon, that I may have the pleasure of seeing you, for I have none to make application to but you alone ; and all I want is, if it was possible you could contrive where I could be employed without going to entire beggary. This probably is a difficult point, yet, unless it's attended with some difficulty, you might think nothing of it, as your long head can bring about matters of much more difficulty and consequence than this.   If you'd disclose this matter to your friend Mr. Buttler, it's possible he might have some employ wherein I could be of use, as I pretend to know as much of breiding and riding of horses as any in France, besides that I am a good hunter, either on horseback or by footing.   You may judge my reduction, as I propose the meanest things to lend a turn till better cast up.   I am sorry that I am obliged to give you so much trouble, but I hope you are very well assured that I am grateful for what you have done for me, and I leave you to judge of my present wretched case.   I am, and shall for ever continue,

"Dear Chief, your own to command,

"JAS. MACGREGOR.

"P.S.—If you'd send your pipes by the bearer, and all the other little trinkims belonging to it, I would put them in order, and play some melancholy tunes, which I may now with safety, and in real truth.   Forgive my not going directly to you, for if I could have borne the seeing of yourself, I could not choose to be seen by my friends in my wretchedness, nor by any of my acquaintance."

While MacGregor wrote in this disconsolate manner, Death, the sad but sure remedy for mortal evils, and decider of all doubts and uncertainties, was hovering near him.   A memorandum on the back of the letter says the writer died about a week after, in October, 1754.

It now remains to mention the fate of Robin Oig, for the other sons of Rob Roy seem to have been no way distinguished.   Robin was apprehended by a party of military from the fort of Inversnaid, at the foot of Gartmore, and was conveyed to Edinburgh 26th May, 1753.   After a delay, which may have been protracted by the negotiations of James for delivering up Allan Breck Stewart, upon promise of his brother's life, Robin Oig, on the 24th December, 1753, was brought to the bar of the High Court of Justiciary, and indicted by the name of Robert MacGregor, *alias* Campbell, *alias* Drummond, *alias* Robert Oig; and the evidence led against him resembled exactly that which was brought by the Crown on the former trial.   Robert's case was in some degree more favourable than his brother's; for, though the principal in the forcible marriage, he had yet to plead that he had shown symptoms of relenting while they were carrying Jean Key off, which were silenced by the remonstrances and threats of his harder natured brother James.   Four years had also elapsed since the poor woman died, which is always a strong circumstance in favour of the accused; for there is a sort of perspective in guilt, and crimes of an old date seem less odious than those of recent occurrence.   But notwithstanding these considerations, the jury, in Robert's case, did not express any solicitude to save his life, as they had done that of James.   They found him guilty of being art and part in the forcible abduction of Jean Key from her own dwelling.*

Robin Oig was condemned to death, and executed on 14th February, 1754. At the place of execution he behaved with great decency; and professing himself a Catholic, imputed all his misfortunes to his swerving from the true church two or three years before. He confessed the violent methods he had used to gain Mrs. Key, or Wright, and hoped his fate would stop further proceedings against his brother James.†

The newspapers observe that his body, after hanging the usual time, was delivered to his friends to be carried to the Highlands. To this the recollection of a venerable friend, recently taken from us in the fulness of years, then a schoolboy at Linlithgow, enables the author to add, that a much larger body of MacGregors than had cared to advance to Edinburgh, received the corpse at that place with the coronach, and other wild emblems of Highland mourning, and so escorted it to Balquhidder. Thus, we may conclude this long account of Rob Roy and his family, with the classic phrase,

"ITE. CONCLAMATUM EST."

I have only to add, that I have selected the above from many anecdotes of Rob Roy, which were, and

* The Trials of the Sons of Rob Roy, with Anecdotes of Himself and his Family, were published at Edinburgh, 1818, in 12mo.

† James died near three months before, but his family might easily remain a long time without the news of that event.

may still be, current among the mountains where he
flourished; but I am far from warranting their exact
authenticity. Clannish partialities were very apt to
guide the tongue and pen as well as the pistol and
claymore, and the features of an anecdote are wonder-
fully softened or exaggerated, as the story is told by a
MacGregor or a Campbell.

APPENDIX.

No. I.

ADVERTISEMENT FOR APPREHENSION

OF

ROB ROY.

(From the Edinburgh Evening Courant, June 18 to June 21, A.D. 1712. No. 1058.)

" THAT Robert Campbell, commonly known by the name of Rob Roy MacGregor, being lately intrusted by several noblemen and gentlemen with considerable sums for buying cows for them in the Highlands, has treacherously gone off with the money, to the value of L.1000 sterling, which he carries along with him. All Magistrates and Officers of his Majesty's forces are intreated to seize upon the said Rob Roy, and the money which he carries with him, until the persons concerned in the money be heard against him ; and that notice be given, when he is apprehended, to the keepers of the Exchange Coffee-house at Edinburgh, and the keeper of the Coffee-house at Glasgow, where the parties concerned will be advertised, and the seizers shall be very reasonably rewarded for their pains."

It is unfortunate that this Hue and Cry, which is afterwards repeated in the same paper, contains no description of Rob Roy's person, which, of course, we must suppose to have been pretty generally known. As it is directed against Rob Roy personally, it would seem to exclude the idea of the cattle being carried off by his partner, MacDonald, who would certainly have been mentioned in the advertisement, if the creditors concerned had supposed him to be in possession of the money.

No. II.

LETTERS

FROM AND TO

THE DUKE OF MONTROSE,

RESPECTING

ROB ROY'S ARREST OF MR. GRAHAME OF KILLEARN.

THE DUKE OF MONTROSE TO————.*

" *Glasgow, the* 21*st November,* 1716.

" MY LORD,—I was surprised last night with the account of a very remarkable instance of the insolence of that very notorious rogue, Rob Roy, whom your lordship has often heard named. The honour of his Majesty's government being concerned in it, I thought it my duty to acquaint your lordship of the particulars by an express.

" Mr. Grahame of Killearn (whom I have had occasion to mention frequently to you, for the good service he did last winter during the rebellion) having the

---

* It does not appear to whom this letter was addressed. Certainly, from its style and tenor, it was designed for some person high in rank and office—perhaps the King's Advocate for the time.

charge of my Highland estate, went to Monteath, which is a part of it, on Monday last, to bring in my rents, it being usual for him to be there for two or three nights together at this time of the year, in a country house, for the conveniency of meeting the tenants, upon that account. The same night, about 9 of the clock, Rob Roy, with a party of those ruffians whom he has still kept about him since the late rebellion, surrounded the house where Mr. Grahame was with some of my tenants doing his business, ordered his men to present their guns in att the windows of the room where he was sitting, while he himself at the same time with others entered at the door, with cocked pistols, and made Mr. Grahame prisoner, carreing him away to the hill with the money he had got, his books and papers, and my tenants' bonds for their fines, amounting to above a thousand pounds sterling, whereof the one half had been paid last year, and the other was to have been paid now; and att the same time had the insolence to cause him to write a letter to me (the copy of which is enclosed) offering me terms of a treaty.

" That your Lordship may have the better view of this matter, it will be necessary that I should inform you, that this fellow has now, of a long time, put himself at the head of the Clan M'Gregor, a race of people who, in all ages, have distinguished themselves beyond others, by robberies, depredations, and murders, and have been the constant harbourers and entertainers of vagabonds and loose people. From the time of the

Revolution he has taken every opportunity to appear against the government, acting rather as a robber than doing any real service to those whom he pretended to appear for, and has really done more mischief to the countrie than all the other Highlanders have done.

"Some three or four years before the last rebellion broke out, being overburdened with debts, he quitted his ordinary residence, and removed some twelve or sixteen miles farther into the Highlands, putting himself under the protection of the Earl of Bredalbin. When my Lord Cadogan was in the Highlands, he ordered his house att this place to be burnt, which your Lordship sees he now places to my account.

"This obliges him to return to the same countrie he went from, being a most rugged inaccessible place, where he took up his residence anew amongst his own friends and relations; but well judging that it was possible to surprise him, he, with about forty-five of his followers, went to Inveraray, and made a sham surrender of their arms to Coll. Campbell of Finab, Commander of one of the Independant Companies, and returned home with his men, each of them having the Coll.'s protection. This happened in the beginning of summer last; yet not long after he appeared with his men twice in arms, in opposition to the King's troops; and one of those times attacked them, rescued a prisoner from them, and all this while sent abroad his party through the countrie, plundering the countrie people, and amongst the rest some of my tenants.

Being informed of these disorders after I came to Scotland, I applied to Lieut. Genll. Carpenter, who ordered three parties from Glasgow, Stirling, and Finlarig, to march in the night by different routes, in order to surprise him and his men in their houses, which would have had its effect certainly, if the great rains that happened to fall that verie night had not retarded the march of the troops, so as some of the parties came too late to the stations that they were ordered for. All that could be done upon the occasion was to burn a countrie house, where Rob Roy then resided, after some of his clan had, from the rocks, fired upon the king's troops, by which a grenadier was killed.

" Mr. Grahame, of Killearn, being my deputy-sheriff in that countrie, went along with the party that marched from Stirling; and, doubtless, will now meet with the worse treatment from that barbarous people on that account. Besides, that he is my relation, and that they know how active he has been in the service of the government—all which, your Lordship may believe, puts me under very great concern for the gentleman, while, at the same time, I can forsee no manner of way how to relieve him, other than to leave him to chance and his own management.

" I had my thoughts before of proposing to govern-ment the building of some barracks, as the only ex-pedient for suppressing these rebels, and securing the peace of the countrie; and in that view I spoke to

Genll. Carpenter, who has now a scheme of it in his hands; and I am persuaded that will be the true method for restraining them effectually; but, in the meantime, it will be necessary to lodge some of the troops in those places, upon which I intend to write to the Generall.

" I am sensible I have troubled your Lordship with a very long letter, which I should be ashamed of, were I myself concerned; but where the honour of the King's Government is touched, I need make no apologie, and I shall only beg leave to add, that I am, with great respect, and truth,

" My Lord,

" yr. Lords^{s.} most humble and

" obedient servant,

" MONTROSE."

218   A P P E N D I X .

COPY OF GRAHAME OF KILLEARN'S LETTER ENCLOSED IN
THE PRECEDING.

"*Chappellaroch, Nov.* 19*th*, 1716.

"MAY IT PLEASE YOUR GRACE,—I am obliged to give
your Grace the trouble of this, by Robert Roy's com-
mands, being so unfortunate at present as to be his
prisoner. I refer the way and manner I was apprehended, to the bearer, and shall only, in short, acquaint
your Grace with the demands, which are, that your
Grace shall discharge him of all soumes he owes your
Grace, and give him the soume of 3400 merks for his
loss and damages sustained by him, both at Craigros-
town and at his house, Auchinchisallen ; and that your
Grace shall give your word not to trouble or prosecute
him afterwards ; till which time he carries me, all the
money I received this day, my books and bonds for
entress, not yet paid, along with him, with assurances
of hard usage, if any party are sent after him. The
soume I received this day, conform to the nearest com-
putation I can make before several of the gentlemen, is
3227L. 2sh. 8d. Scots, of which I gave them notes. I
shall wait your Grace's return, and ever am,

"Your Grace's most obedient, faithful,
"humble servant,

Sic subscribitur,   "JOHN GRAHAME."

THE DUKE OF MONTROSE TO ———.

28th Nov. 1716.—KILLEARN'S RELEASE.

"*Glasgow, 28th Nov.* 1716.

"SIR,—Having acquainted you by my last, of the 21st instant, of what had happened to my friend Mr. Grahame of Killearn, I'm very glad now to tell you, that last night I was very agreeably surprised with Mr. Grahame's coming here himself, and giving me the first account I had had of him from the time of his being carried away. It seems Rob Roy, when he came to consider a little better of it, found that he could not mend his matters by retaining Killearn his prisoner, which could only expose him still the more to the justice of the government; and therefore thought fit to dismiss him on Sunday evening last, having kept him from the Monday night before, under a very uneasy kind of restraint, being obliged to change continually from place to place. He gave him back the books, papers, and bonds, but kept the money.

"I am, with great truth, Sir,
"your most humble servant,
"MONTROSE."

No. III.

CHALLENGE BY ROB ROY.

ROB ROY *to ain hie and mighty Prince,* JAMES DUKE OF MONTROSE.

" In charity to your Grace's couradge and conduct, please know, the only way to retrieve both is to treat Rob Roy like himself, in appointing your place and choice of arms, that at once you may extirpate your inveterate enemy, or put a period to your punny (puny?) life in falling gloriously by his hands. That impertinent criticks or flatterer's may not brand me for challenging a man that's repute of a poor dastardly soul, let such know that I admit of the two great supporters of his character and the captain of his bands to joyne with him in the combate. Then sure your Grace will not have the impudence to clamour att court for multitudes to hunt me like a fox, under pretence that I am not to be found above ground. This saves your Grace and the troops any further trouble of searching ; that is, if your ambition of glory press you to embrace this unequald venture offerd of Rob's head. But if your Grace's piety, prudence, and cowardice, forbids hazarding this gentlemanly expedient, then let your design of peace restore what you have robed from me by the

tyranny of your present cituation, otherwise your over-
throw as a man is determined; and advertise your
friends never more to look for the frequent civility
payed them, of sending them home without their arms
only. Even their former cravings wont purchase that
favour; so your Grace by this has peace in your offer,
if the sound of war be frightful, and chuse your whilk,
your good friend or mortal enemy."

[This singular rhodomotade is enclosed in a letter to
a friend of Rob Roy, probably a retainer of the Duke
of Argyle in Isla, which is in these words :—]

"SIR,—Receive the enclosed paper, q^n you are taking
your botle; it will divert yourself and comrades. I got
noa news since I saw you, only q^t we had before about
the Spanyards is like to continue. If I get any account
about them I'll be sure to let you hear of it, and till
then I will not write any more till I have more account.
I am, Sir, your affec C^n [cousin,] and most humble
servant,

"*Argyle*, 1719.   "ROB ROY."

Addressed, To Mr. Patrick Anderson, }
    at Haig—These.   }
The seal, a stag—no bad emblem }
    of a wild catteran.   }

It appears from the envelope that Rob Roy still continued to act as an intelligencer to the Duke of Argyle and his agents. The war he alludes to is probably some vague report of invasion from Spain. Such rumours were likely enough to be afloat, in consequence of the disembarkation of the troops who were taken at Glensheal in the preceding year, 1718.

———

No. IV.

FROM ROBERT CAMPBELL, ALIAS M'GREGOR,
COMMONLY CALLED ROB ROY,

TO FIELD-MARSHAL WADE,

*Then receiving the submission of disaffected Chieftains and Clans.**

"SIR,—The great humanity with which you have constantly acted in discharge of the trust reposed in you, and your ever having made use of the great powers with which you were vested, as the means of doing good and charitable offices to such as ye found

* This curious epistle is copied from an authentic narrative of Marshal Wade's proceedings in the Highlands, communicated by the late eminent antiquary, George Chalmers, Esq., to Mr. Robert Jamieson of the Register House, Edinburgh, and published in the Appendix to an Edition of Burt's Letters from the North of Scotland. 2 Vols., 8vo. Edinburgh, 1818.

proper objects of compassion, will, I hope, excuse my importunity in endeavouring to approve myself not absolutely unworthy of that mercy and favour which your Excellency has so generously procured from his Majesty for others in my unfortunate circumstances. I am very sensible nothing can be alledged sufficient to excuse so great a crime as I have been guilty of, that of Rebellion. But I humbly beg leave to lay before your Excellency some particulars in the circumstance of my guilt, which, I hope, will extenuate it in some measure. It was my misfortune, at the time the Rebellion broke out, to be liable to legal diligence and caption, at the Duke of Montrose's instance, for debt alledged due to him. To avoid being flung into prison, as I must certainly have been, had I followed my real inclinations in joining the King's troops at Stirling, I was forced to take party with the adherents of the Pretender; for the country being all in arms, it was neither safe nor indeed possible for me to stand neuter. I should not, however, plead my being forced into that unnatural Rebellion against his Majesty, King George, if I could not at the same time assure your Excellency, that I not only avoided acting offensively against his Majesty's forces upon all occasions, but on the contrary, sent his Grace the Duke of Argyle all the intelligence I could from time to time, of the strength and situation of the Rebels; which I hope his Grace will do me the justice to acknowledge. As to the debt to the Duke of Montrose, I have discharged it to the utmost farthing, I beg your Excellency would be persuaded that, had it been in my power, as it was in my inclination, I should always have acted for the service of his Majesty King George, and that one reason of my begging the favour of your intercession with his Majesty for the pardon of my life, is the earnest desire I have to employ it in his service, whose goodness, justice, and humanity, are so conspicuous to all mankind.

> "I am, with all duty and respect,
> "Your Excellency's most, etc.
>
> "ROBERT CAMPBELL."

No. V.

ON HIGHLAND WOOING.

There are many productions of the Scottish Ballad Poets upon the lion-like mode of wooing practised by the ancient Highlanders when they had a fancy for the person (or property) of a Lowland damsel. One example is found in Mr. Robert Jamieson's Popular Scottish Songs:—

> Bonny Babby Livingstone
> Gaed out to see the kye,
> And she has met with Glenlyon,
> Who has stolen her away.

> He took frae her her satin coat,
>   But an her silken gown,
> Syne roud her in his tartan plaid,
>   And happd her round and roun'.

In another ballad we are told how

> Four-and-twenty Hieland men
>   Came doun by Fiddoch side,
> And they have sworn a deadly aith,
>   Jean Muir suld be a bride :
>
> And they have sworn a deadly aith,
>   Ilke man upon his durke,
> That she should wed with Duncan Ger,
>   Or they'd make bloody worke.

This last we have from tradition, but there are many others in the collections of Scottish Ballads to the same purpose.

The achievement of Robert Oig, or young Rob Roy, as the Lowlanders called him, was celebrated in a ballad, of which there are twenty different and various editions. The tune is lively and wild, and we select the following words from memory :

> Rob Roy is frae the Hielands come,
>   Down to the Lowland border ;
> And he has stolen that lady away,
>   To haud his house in order.
>
> He set her on a milk-white steed,
>   Of none he stood in awe ;
> Untill they reached the Hieland hills,
>   Aboon the Balmaha' ! *
>
> Saying, Be content, be content,
>   Be content with me, lady ;

---

* A pass on the eastern margin of Loch Lomond, and an entrance to the Highlands.

Where will ye find in Lennox land,
  Sae braw a man as me, lady ?

Rob Roy, he was my father called,
  MacGregor was his name, Lady ;
A' the country, far and near,
  Have heard MacGregor's fame, lady.

He was a hedge about his friends,
  A heckle to his foes, lady ;
If any man did him gainsay,
  He felt his deadly blows, lady.

I am as bold, I am as bold,
  I am as bold and more, lady ;
Any man that doubts my word,
  May try my gude claymore, lady.

Then be content, be content,
  Be content with me, lady ;
For now you are my wedded wife,
  Until the day ye die, lady.

No. VI.

GHLUNE DHU.

THE following notices concerning this Chief fell under the Author's eye while the sheets were in the act of going through the press. They occur in manuscript memoirs, written by a person intimately acquainted with the incidents of 1745.

This Chief had the important task intrusted to him of defending the castle of Doune, in which the Chevalier placed a garrison to protect his communication with the Highlands, and to repel any sallies which might be made from Stirling Castle. Ghlune Dhu distinguished himself by his good conduct in this charge.

Ghlune Dhu is thus described :—" Glengyle is, in person, a tall handsome man, and has more of the mien of the ancient heroes than our modern fine gentlemen are possessed of. He is honest and disinterested to a proverb—extremely modest—brave and intrepid—and born one of the best partisans in Europe. In short, the whole people of that country declared that never did men live under so mild a government as Glengyle's, not a man having so much as lost a chicken while he continued there."

It would appear from this curious passage that Glengyle—not Stewart of Balloch, as averred in a note on Waverley—commanded the garrison of Doune. Balloch might, no doubt, succeed MacGregor in the situation.

DATE DUE			

F
Hob

Hobbs, Will 21149

Far North